PRECEDENTS

AND

PROMISE

IN THE CURRICULUM FIELD

PRECEDENTS

AND

PROMISE

IN THE CURRICULUM FIELD

Helen F. Robison

Editor

TEACHERS COLLEGE PRESS

Teachers College • Columbia University

Cover design by Veit-Martin Associates

EDITOR'S PREFACE

A DECADE AGO, curriculum designers were educators and curriculum critics were not. Today, however, criticism is being heard on all sides *within* the curriculum field of the many new designs which have originated from *outside* sources. With the pendulum now at the other extreme, the committee for the 1965 Curriculum Conference chose to focus on an analysis of the development of the curriculum field, or its precedents, the nature of emerging and converging trends today, and the promise for the near future. To this end, educators from all over North America met at a three-day conference, at Teachers College, Columbia University, on November 8, 9, and 10, to hear some major presentations on these topics and to discuss the pressing problems of curriculum workers today.

If a single theme could be identified from several dominant *leitmotifs* developed in the individual papers, it would be the need for humanizing the curriculum, for harnessing technology and all other curriculum determiners to serve human purposes. The individual was viewed not only in his uniqueness, but as one with all other persons, in a human struggle to find meaning and self-actualization through self-chosen purposes and relevant educational experiences. It is surely no accident that morality, justice, and educational values were seen as opposed to a means-ends conception of the curriculum and as transcending neat and narrow packages of delimited content for standarized objectives. Population pressures and automation have stirred curriculum designers to intensify their value commitments to the person, in the face of an escalating cult of efficiency and depersonalization. On the night of November 9, the conference participants experienced the gigantic power failure which blacked out almost the entire Northeast, projecting an example, if one were needed, of the transcendance of human dignity and human values over technology.

Other themes identified the need for a theoretical framework from which rational analysis and evaluation of new curriculum proposals and designs could be made. The central position of curriculum workers was emphasized by several speakers who urged the importance of mediating proposals coming from all directions without regard to the effects upon children and schools. Openness to new ideas and to collaboration with personnel from the many areas now contributing to curriculum pervaded the papers, along with analyses of previous cycles of change in curriculum design.

The promise of progress in the curriculum field in the near future was attributed to current widespread public interest, the new federal financial support and the commitment of leadership from many contiguous areas. With caution for the human values which are endangered by many trends in the contemporary scene, the conference speakers voiced guarded optimism for real progress in the curriculum field in the next few years.

This publication includes the seven presentations which were made in general sessions, in addition to the two made simultaneously by Margaret Lindsey and Joseph O. Loretan on the final day, in two separate sessions, with about half the conference participants in each group. Afternoon discussion groups explored the implications of these presentations for various levels in schools, for the varieties of school populations served and for special problems of concern today. Implications for curriculum implementation and for teacher education were analyzed by many groups. The three hundred and fifty conference participants, who came from all sections of the United States, and from Canada, brought a wide range of their own concerns and interests into their discussions of the conference papers and reports.

I am indebted to the many doctoral students in the Department of Curriculum and Teaching who assisted in recording the issues and questions dealt with in the group discussions. I wish also to express my appreciation to Dorothy Pritchett, Conference Secretary, who assisted in preparing this manuscript.

Finally, I must acknowledge my indebtedness to those who made this conference possible, especially its initial chairman, Arthur J. Lewis, and committee members Alice Miel and Leland B. Jacobs. Two other committee members who assisted in the earlier planning phase were Stephen M. Corey and Dwayne Huebner.

HELEN F. ROBISON
Assistant Professor of Education
Teachers College, Columbia University

CONTENTS

vii

EMERGENCE OF THE CURRICULUM AS A FIELD OF PROFESSIONAL WORK AND STUDY

Hollis L. Caswell

THE CURRICULUM has been a subject of study and innovation since the beginning of organized education. Innumerable historical events and persons have contributed to its present form and content. Names such as Comenius, Pestalozzi, Herbart, Froebel, Horace Mann, and William T. Harris are reminders that serious thought about the curriculum and extensive efforts to achieve new and better forms have been an ever-present characteristic of Western education.

Emergence of the curriculum as a distinctive field of professional activity occurred around 1920. In 1918 Professor Franklin Bobbitt of the University of Chicago published the first general book on the subject.[1] In 1920 in Los Angeles he directed the first city system-wide program of curriculum revision. Earlier, supervisors and administrators had written courses of study on a piecemeal basis. Preparation of supervisory personnel to write curricula was a secondary goal in courses on supervision, such as the one given by Professor Frank McMurry at Teachers College, Columbia University. Professor Bobbitt took the major step of dealing with the curriculum in all subjects and grades on a unified and comprehensive basis.

In 1922 Denver inaugurated a system-wide program of curriculum revision. About that time Winnetka, Illinois, launched a series of intensive research studies that laid the basis for its distinctive curriculum approach

---

[1] Franklin Bobbitt, *The Curriculum* (Boston: Houghton Mifflin, 1918).

HOLLIS L. CASWELL is President Emeritus of Teachers College, Columbia University.

emphasizing individual pupil progress. The next large-scale, system-wide revision program to attract nationwide attention was in St. Louis. In 1925 a major effort was initiated there involving the work of several hundred teachers and the assistance of a large group of specialists as consultants. Within two years new courses of study were prepared in all elementary and secondary school subjects.

During this period of activity in city school systems two further developments helped establish the curriculum as a field of professional study. First, several major books on the subject were published. Of special importance in the early years of the movement was a comprehensive analysis by W. W. Charters of The Ohio State University, published in 1923 under the title *Curriculum Construction*.[2] Second, curriculum laboratories were organized. The first was at Teachers College, Columbia University, and was established in 1926 under the direction of Herbert Bruner with Florence Stratemeyer as associate.

Thus curriculum revision became a matter of wide interest. Study and field activity rapidly expanded. In 1926, the National Society for the Study of Education published a major review of the movement, devoting both parts of its yearbook[3] to the subject. The report was prepared by a distinguished committee under the chairmanship of Harold Rugg. This book gives the best presently available account of the early development of the organized curriculum movement. By 1930, state departments of education had become seriously interested in comprehensive programs of curriculum improvement. The first such programs were in South Dakota and Alabama. The most widely known and generally influential one was in Virginia. Within the decade many states undertook programs. Also during the 1930's the Eight-Year Study of the Progressive Education Association stimulated curriculum revision.

State curriculum programs took the lead in making a highly important redefinition of the meaning of the curriculum. Whereas earlier work accepted the traditional concept of the curriculum as consisting of a group of courses of study, leaders of state programs came to view the curriculum operationally, considering it to be composed of the experiences pupils actually had under the guidance of the school. Earlier, efforts were directed primarily to writing consistent, good documents. When they were pub-

---

2 W. W. Charters, *Curriculum Construction* (New York: Macmillan, 1923).

3 Harold Rugg (Ed.), *The Foundations and Technique of Curriculum Construction,* Twenty-sixth Yearbook of the National Society for the Study of Education (Bloomington, Ill.: Public School Publishing Co., 1926).

lished, it became the responsibility of the supervisory staff to get classroom teachers to follow them. It soon became evident that this was no simple task. Elaborate arrangements for the preparation of courses of study by committees composed of representatives of classroom teachers were designed, and extensive plans were made for installation of the resulting courses of study by supervisors and principals. But even so, leaders in state curriculum programs became aware that these revised courses of study did not as a rule lead to changes in classroom practice. Courses of study gathered dust on shelves. It became increasingly clear that revision of the curriculum should have the central purpose of modifying instruction, and that curriculum programs must utilize many means to achieve this end in addition to writing courses of study. The Florida state curriculum program in 1930 was the first to adopt as its central purpose the improvement of instruction and to start its work with an in-service study program for all teachers in the state. The Virginia program greatly extended this approach. General acceptance of this pragmatic emphasis came quite quickly.

Two events were of special importance. One was the organization at Teachers College, Columbia University, of the Department of Curriculum and Teaching in 1937. This largely grew out of the insight of Jesse H. Newlon, who, as Superintendent of Schools, had been instrumental in initiating the curriculum program in Denver in 1922. The Department of Curriculum and Teaching drew together work and staff from seven older departments to deal at all school and college levels with what had previously been classified as curriculum, supervision, general methods, materials of teaching, and in-service education. The other event of great importance was the establishment of the Association for Supervision and Curriculum Development. Curriculum workers had previously belonged to the Society for Curriculum Study, and supervisory personnel to the Department of Supervisors and Directors of Instruction. The new association brought all together in a working group and set instructional improvements as a common goal.

Paralleling this development was a gradual shift in administrative organization in state and city school systems to insure a unified and consistent curriculum, extending from the kindergarten through the high school. In 1930 the State Superintendent in Virginia organized all curriculum and supervisory personnel in a single administrative unit under the direction of a major officer. Gradually other systems began to change so that by the close of the decade there was wide acceptance of the concept that all work relating to the curriculum and instruction should be unified under the guidance of a single administrator.

CRITICISM AND PERSISTENCE OF THE MOVEMENT

In its beginning the curriculum movement, like all new approaches in education, had its critics, and from time to time it has experienced rough going. In 1934 William C. Bagley, in his book entitled *Education and Emergent Man,* wrote a section headed, "The Golden Decade: Curriculum Experts, Curriculum Committees, Curriculum Chaos." He stated, following discussion of developments from 1912 to 1920:

> Then came a series of events that resulted in a state of confusion which persists at the time of the present writing. Several persons began to make the study of the total school curriculum problem their special field—which is a large order for any one person to undertake. It was not long before the reconstruction of curricula became the educational fashion. . . . The movement spread rapidly . . . and by 1933 there were no fewer than 35,000 different curricula on file in the curriculum laboratory of Teachers College, Columbia University. . . .[4]

Bagley was by no means alone in his criticism of curriculum revision by local school systems. Many saw the curriculum as such a broad and indefinite area of study that no individual could develop expertness in it. Others felt that only subject matter specialists had significant contributions to make. Many considered the work of classroom teachers in curriculum planning so naive as not to merit attention in a serious educational endeavor. Yet the movement thrived. More and more school systems accepted it as essential that they have a system-wide, organized curriculum program; more and more schools of education included courses on the curriculum in their offerings; more and more books and articles and research studies were written about curriculum development.

The movement has now persisted for nearly a half century. During this time many educational practices have come and gone—and some have even had a rebirth. Ability grouping was considered a panacea by many during the late twenties. Yet under the impact of extensive research it practically disappeared from the educational scene until its recent resurrection in the hope that it would foster academic excellence. The Platoon School was a widely popular plan of curriculum and school organization in many of our large cities for years. A national association fostered its development. Yet it is gone, with hardly a vestige remaining. The activity curriculum had a large group of ardent followers among both educators and laymen. It would now be a courageous person who proposed to a community that its schools follow this plan. These and other educational practices have developed

---

[4] William C. Bagley, *Education and Emergent Man* (New York: Thomas Nelson and Sons, 1934), p. 140.

and disappeared during the period that the curriculum movement has spread from one school system to another.

Why is this the case? Why have curriculum activity, study, and research persisted? In answering this question we can clarify and rededicate ourselves to the areas of study which the curriculum should encompass and to the kinds of competence curriculum workers should possess.

MATTERS OF CENTRAL CONCERN

Within the limits of this paper it is possible to sketch only briefly some of the central concerns of the curriculum as it has emerged as a recognized field of professional activity and study. There are a number of basic educational problems that I believe are the central responsibility of curriculum workers, for they alone are in a position to resolve them effectively. This is the reason, as I see it, that the curriculum as an area of study has persisted in programs of professional education, and why school systems have increasingly devoted personnel and money to curriculum work. By way of illustration, I shall discuss briefly three problem areas that have been persistent concerns through most or all of the curriculum movement.

Goals, purposes, objectives, or aims of education—terms which I shall use synonymously in this discussion—represent one major area of curriculum concern. This is not to imply by any means that these are exclusively the concern of curriculum workers. It is from goals, purposes, or aims that education achieves direction. If goals are lacking in clarity, breadth, or consistency the educational program will lack these same qualities. No educational worker should be unconcerned about goals, for in every activity from planning a school building to teaching a class, goals are implicit, recognized or not. A central concern of philosophers is values, and values provide the basis for selecting goals. But goals of education as stated by philosophers are general in nature. They suggest the direction education should take but leave a great gap which must be filled if teachers and students are to have meaningful guidance for day-by-day activities. The fundamental problem facing curriculum specialists is to establish a consistent relationship between general goals, on the one hand, and specific objectives that guide teaching, on the other.

Good teaching requires a strong sense of purpose. If the student is to have maximum opportunity to achieve the general goals of education, the teacher must understand how each specific objective fits into a configuration of purposes which, in time, tie into a coordinated developmental sequence. To define and formulate goals of education so that they are truly operational guides to teaching is a difficult task and one that should always be central in curriculum work. Unless this is well done the educational program will lack consistency and cumulative effect.

The Los Angeles curriculum program in 1920 was the first instance in which an effort was made to formulate a series of teaching objectives in the various subjects that were developmental in nature and contributed consistently to centrally-held educational goals. The St. Louis program in 1926 went further in a thorough treatment of this problem. During this period substantial research studies such as Billings' on generalizations basic to the social studies[5] and reports such as those from Winnetka provided useful information.

For many years the translation of aims of education into operational guides for teaching was recognized as a central curriculum problem. Of late it has received much less attention. This is of critical importance when you consider the nature of our times. We are in a period in which values are being questioned, in which teaching practice has undergone great change, in which a vast array of new content has arisen, in which the demands of society upon schools have increased with each passing year, and in which goals of education are a major source of controversy. It is my judgment that curriculum workers neglect a principal responsibility when they fail to give major attention to research and practice that help clarify the goals education should serve, that interpret these goals into specific objectives which serve as operationally effective guides to teaching, and that foster consistency among the various phases of the curriculum.

The next major area of concern to which I direct your attention is the problem commonly referred to as assuring sound sequence or continuity in the curriculum. This problem was foreshadowed by the work of certain national committees following 1910. Reports of these committees reflected general concern among professional educators about the disjointed way in which the curriculum was organized. I refer especially to the Committee on Economy of Time established in 1911, which made four reports over a period of eight years, and to work on articulation. A strong feeling existed that the educational program was not organized to achieve the greatest cumulative effect in pupil achievement and the most economical learning. One of the most important elements contributing to this concern was the fact that the curriculums at the elementary and secondary school levels and in the various subjects were planned with little reference to each other. There was great concern also about the gap between high school and college work.

Early curriculum programs made a direct attack on this problem at the

5 Neal Billings, *A Determination of Generalizations Basic to the Social Studies Curriculum* (Baltimore: Warwick and York, 1929).

school level by a deductive procedure for deriving objectives for each unit of instruction in each grade and each subject from general aims of education. It was believed that through such a procedure the problem would be solved for the school program because continuity would be assured from the first grade through high school and consistency of objectives for different subjects would be established.

After a decade of work it became apparent that other factors than aims were involved in developing a curriculum that provided the desired articulation or sequential relationships. Personal and social problems, the developmental characteristics of pupils, the essential interrelationships of facts, methods of work, and concepts in various subject matter fields, and the influence of out-of-school situations on school experience were recognized as additional important factors. Consequently in the 1930's the problem of articulation was defined more broadly as the problem of sequence. Various plans were devised and put to trial to assure a curriculum sequence that effectively took into account these several factors. Fusion of subjects was tried, sequences of large units of work were developed, the social-functions approach with emphasis on persistent problems of living was devised, and the core curriculum plan was created. None of these attempts to devise a new and more effective procedure for defining sequence met with outstanding success. Gradually the problem came to be described as one of providing continuity in the curriculum, a definition that brought the problem closer to classroom practice. It continued to be studied by curriculum workers, but no significantly new and more satisfactory methods have been developed by which appropriate emphasis can be given in curriculum planning to the three basic factors involved: (1) the potentialities of the learner and his already acquired interests, attitudes, and knowledge, (2) personal and social problems wherein learnings become dynamic, meaningful, and useful, and (3) the organization of knowledge so that the learner gains in power and depth of understanding, and masters methods of work that provide him the most reliable means that he can command to meet new situations.

At the present time the dominant influence is the same as operated during the period from 1890 to 1920. Once again national committees are devising new programs in subject matter fields for the secondary school. As in the earlier period we are now starting at the top and working down. Already considerable curriculum revision at the elementary school level is done more with the idea of building down from the high school program than because studies of elementary-aged children indicate the changes are desirable. Even so, the full impact of this trend has not yet been felt. Another likeness is that present revision is carried forward primarily by subject specialists from graduate faculties of universities. Still another likeness is that work in the various subjects is done with little regard for what the total curriculum should encompass. This piecemeal approach led to the fragmented program that was considered a major weakness in earlier years.

Continuity is now of even greater importance than in the past. With the tremendous increase in knowledge, specialization has become even greater. Yet, important advances in knowledge which are of great general social significance occur very frequently where fields cross; in other words, interdisciplinary relationships are of increasing importance. Thus the challenging concerns of the great group of subject specialists move further away from using the knowledge in their fields to help solve the problems non-specialists encounter in daily life. Concern for general education wanes, and we begin preparing mathematicians, physicists, and chemists in the elementary school. The problems of the citizen, the homemaker, the person with leisure time, and youth unable to get jobs swamp our society; but these problems are given short shrift by many of those who exert great influence on the curriculum of American schools today.

In the period following 1910 academic scholars such as James Harvey Robinson, Alfred North Whitehead, and Charles Beard, as well as professional students of education, recognized the weaknesses of the fragmented curriculum that had resulted from subject matter committees building from the top down with little if any concern for developmental characteristics of students and for those general life situations in which knowledge functions. There is no reason that a curriculum so designed today will have any more felicitous results. In fact, Dr. Alvin Weinberg, Director of the Oak Ridge National Laboratory, this past summer characterized the work of national committees in the new mathematics and the sciences as dangerous, calling the curriculum plans they have developed "puristic monsters." The root of the problem, he holds, is control by university specialists whose central concern is purity of concept, which leads to remoteness from everyday life.[6] This is the same criticism made earlier by James Harvey Robinson and the others to whom I have just referred.

This problem of developing a truly sequential curriculum must be approached with a view of the total educational offering. Those who solve it must see across subject and grade and school boundaries. They must be able to build a whole of educational experience that is larger than the sum of its parts because of the mutual support and interrelationship of the parts. Only general curriculum workers are in a position to discharge this responsibility. Others must of course contribute, but no one

6 *The New York Times,* August 6, 1965.

else has the freedom from vested interest to look impartially at the competing claims of various groups of specialists and to balance these interests in terms of the best service to students and society.

A third major area of study that is a distinctive responsibility of general curriculum workers is that of balance in the educational offering. The curriculum through the years has developed by a process of accretion. As new fields have arisen their proponents have had to fight hard to secure a place for them in the school offering. The result has been that the curriculum is largely a patchwork. The emphasis given to various studies is determined substantially by historical accident and by the relative strength of the competing supporters of various subjects.

The only way out of this difficulty is to employ a procedure that provides for an impartial review of the educational potentialities of all fields of study at each level of instruction, and that formulates a guiding set of priorities. These priorities should not be determined by special interest group pressures, legislative action, or the particular likes and dislikes of teachers but rather by analysis of the comparative contribution of each to the growth of individual students and to social well-being. Knowledge of developmental psychology, of national goals, of the potential contribution of various subjects, and of the teaching-learning process must be brought together in consistent criteria applied to determine such a set of priorities and to formulate a plan of curriculum organization.

Subject specialists should have an important part in this process, for they can best identify the potentialities of their fields for student growth. But much more is needed. The specialist in developmental psychology, in goals of education, and in teaching-learning procedures should also be involved. It is the task of the general curriculum worker to bring together the knowledge of these specialists in a manner which will afford a reasoned basis for determining *how much of what* shall be included in the curriculum at various levels of study. The outcome desired is a curriculum design which provides a reasoned balance of emphasis upon various areas of study for given students.

General curriculum workers should now take hold of this problem with much greater vigor. They should attack the study of design at the level to which the Educational Policies Commission had brought it in *Education for All American Youth;* they should examine carefully the work of subject committees of recent years to discover those ideas and techniques which hold significance for designing a consistent, balanced total program; they should study field programs such as the one in North Carolina where practitioners have gone forward in developing an outstanding program in occupational preparation along with a strengthened academic offering. From these sources and from analyses of national conditions and the needs and problems of children and youth, they should project new and improved curriculum designs. If the general curriculum worker does not deal with balance and priorities, nobody else will, and we shall continue to have a curriculum in our schools that is a patchwork, rather than one planned on the basis of a broad and fundamental view of the kind of education our nation and our people need in the kind of world in which we now live.

SOME GENERAL CONCLUSIONS

Viewing the emergence of the organized curriculum movement with present perspective, there are several general conclusions that I offer for your consideration:

1. The organized curriculum movement has the central purpose of avoiding a fragmented, out-of-date curriculum that is shaped by competing special interest groups. It seeks to develop instead a program which supports common objectives throughout and which is characterized by a balanced emphasis on the several areas of study and various types of pupil activities. It seeks also to guide pupils into experiences that are appropriate to their developmental characteristics, challenging to their interests, and which relate constructively to significant social conditions and needs.
2. The persistence of important professional problems that are studied systematically only by general curriculum workers has made the curriculum a field of established professional importance.
3. During the course of the curriculum movement, the extension of the concept of curriculum development from writing courses of study to that of affording new and more educationally desirable experiences for students has had a profound effect on the scope and activities of curriculum programs. It has led to general acceptance of the idea that classroom teachers generally must take a major part in curriculum programs since change in practice depends upon their ability and willingness to modify existing teaching procedures.
4. Comprehensive curriculum programs—especially since the early ones such as at Denver and St. Louis—have not generally made optimum use of subject specialists. As a result activities and subject matter that are most educationally desirable often have not been included in the curriculum.
5. The plans of organization of a large proportion of curriculum programs have been too narrow and rigid to encompass the varied pupil activities and subject matter essential to meet the wide range of aptitudes and

abilities in a school serving all the children of all the people. The result has been that important educational needs of both students and society have been neglected. A curriculum that challenges the abilities and meets the needs of a student who has the promise of becoming a productive, creative scholar in an academic field, and which also provides for a pupil with below average verbal ability who has the promise of becoming a responsible and efficient worker in one of the skilled trades, must provide wide scope and great flexibility in organization.

6. We have not defined with sufficient preciseness the areas of study which are encompassed in the curriculum as a field of professional work, nor developed through research and carefully evaluated practice an adequate body of knowledge which clearly demonstrates the significance of the field.

7. A major source of strength in the curriculum movement has been a persistent concern for improvement of the process of curriculum change. From activity and job analysis, contract plans, and fusion of subjects into broad fields, through analysis of social life into areas of living, and other approaches, the central concern has been to develop a process which would lead to the actual improvement of learning experiences for students. Thus the movement has been characterized both by persistence of a dominant purpose and flexibility of method.

In conclusion, I have undertaken through this analysis of the emergence of the curriculum movement to show that those who work on the curriculum have a highly important professional responsibility to discharge. The modern curriculum movement has survived doubts; it has gone through troubled times. The greatest test lies just ahead. If the movement is to continue and grow in strength and effectiveness, it will require wisdom, hard work, and readiness to seek new and better means of enlisting the cooperative action of all those who have an interest in the curriculum. Above all it will require a level of professional dedication that imbues curriculum workers with the courage to insist that their voices be heard in the councils of those groups that shape the future of our educational system.

THE CURRICULUM
FIELD TODAY

Kenneth D. Wann

It would be naive to believe that it is possible within the scope of this brief paper to present a comprehensive account of current developments in the curriculum field. So much is happening that it would be difficult merely to inventory the activities. To present a careful analysis would be impossible. Consequently, I have chosen to identify certain characteristics and problems of the current scene which I believe are of special concern to those of us here today who work as curriculum specialists in schools of education or in public school systems.

A dominant factor in American education today is a curriculum reform movement which seems to be moving toward an almost complete transformation of classrooms at all levels. Gathering momentum since the launching of Sputnik I, the movement encompasses hundreds of proposals for reforms in content and methodology for the teaching of mathematics, the physical sciences, the social sciences, and the humanities at all levels from nursery school through college.

Curriculum innovation is newsworthy today although it does not occupy the prominent position in the nation's press of other educational problems and concerns. Racial and religious controversy in education rightfully continues to command headline space. Nevertheless, prominence is given to many curriculum innovations. Most newspapers have carried numerous items on such innovations as the new mathematics, the initial teaching alphabet, and teaching machines. Few people in this country have not read in the press of Project Head Start and the proposals for providing

Kenneth D. Wann is Professor of Education at Teachers College, Columbia University.

early learning experiences for the large segment of our population designated as disadvantaged.

This general concern suggests a significant characteristic of the curriculum reform movement of the 1960's—the great interest of many groups outside of the field of professional education in curriculum innovation. In many respects, the current efforts toward reform might be considered a popular movement. Proposals for innovation are coming from many sources. Lay groups, social reformers, psychologists and medical people, subject matter specialists, philanthropic foundations, government agencies, to mention only a few sources, are exercising powerful influences for change.

This widespread popular interest in curriculum innovation brings excitement and vitality to curriculum development today. It also brings problems of considerable magnitude. Each of the groups advocating change has its particular axe to grind, and usually a proposed reform is not viewed in relation to other proposed reforms. Under the continuing influence of such change tactics, the curriculum as developed in American schools can become an even more hopeless hodgepodge of diverse goals and procedures than it now is.

Two years ago John Goodlad characterized the curriculum scene in a sentence. "This is a historic point in educational development," he said, "not because of any one event or reform, but because so many things are happening at the same time and a lot of them fit together."[1] It is when the reforms fit together that real progress is made. It is when they do not fit, and unfortunately, many do not, that we grow concerned about the impact of a patchwork curriculum upon learners.

A case in point is the subject-by-subject examination of curriculum content which is underway by groups of specialists representing the academic disciplines. There is, no doubt, an urgent need for careful study and clarification of the inherent logic of each subject and the ends for which a student pursues a study of the subject. Unnecessary fragmentation of the curriculum for learners occurs, however, when the proposals of these separate groups are installed as curriculum content without reference to the total impact on students.

A second characteristic of the current curriculum reform movement is the emphasis on speed of change. A sense of urgency to make rapid progress pervades the entire social scene. Schools, feeling a need to move in response to the times, often adopt programs and practices which have little to support them other than the arguments of their advocates. In the urgency to move ahead, inadequate provisions are made for systematic evaluation of

[1] As quoted in Lawrence A. Cremin, "Focus on Education," *The World Book Yearbook* (Chicago: Field Enterprises Educational Corporation, 1964), p. 38.

the impact the changes make on learners and learning. Furthermore, the speed with which some proposed programs are adopted precludes adequate preparation of teachers for implementing the changes in sound teaching practices.

Often the innovation comes in the form of a packaged curriculum which is designed to be as nearly "teacher proof" as possible. In view of the speed with which school systems adopt such programs this tightly structured approach to change may be desirable. To present teachers with specific teaching goals and a set of materials guaranteed to achieve the goals when used according to directions may seem to eliminate the need for more than a token orientation to new approaches, but such a practice leaves little room for individual teacher initiative. Such inflexibility increases the frustration of the creative, able teachers we so desperately need in our schools. And more significantly, the packaged curriculum approach leaves little room for flexibility in adapting content and methods to the special needs of individual learners or groups of learners.

It is a well known fact that some of the widely used programs in mathematics and science have been developed with special groups of learners, usually the very bright. These programs were not tested widely before their adoption by schools for use with a normal range of learners. As a consequence serious frustration on the part of teachers and pupils has resulted.

A third characteristic of the curriculum reform movement is the imposition of changes in curriculum content onto an existing pattern of school organization. The national committees involved in curriculum reform have proceeded on the assumption that the organization of schools in terms of class size, pupil-teacher ratio, staff deployment, instructional time, and course organization would remain the same. In a sense, the proposed innovations in curriculum content have frozen present school organization and have given tacit support to the status quo in an area seriously in need of careful scrutiny in relation to curriculum change.

It is interesting, to say the least, in the recent history of educational reform that we have not been able to get proposed changes in organization and in curriculum working together. The proposals of the late 1950's for team teaching, ungraded schools, and homogeneous grouping of pupils were made with little concern for the necessary concomitant changes in content and methodology, whereas, today, we consider changes in content with little concern for the changes necessary in organization.

This brief indication of the way this commentator views current curriculum development suggests a number of problems and needs which demand the attention of curriculum workers. I believe that the problems are of such magnitude as to demand concerted effort among curriculum specialists.

NEED FOR LEADERSHIP IN CURRICULUM DEVELOPMENT

It is readily apparent that there is need for firm and even aggressive leadership by curriculum specialists in developing curriculums that will be appropriate for today's children in today's world. One of the facts of today's situation is the loss of the initiative and leadership in curriculum development by the group of people who have the expertise to mediate knowledge from the many areas impinging on curriculum development. Curriculum specialists often find themselves trailing the pack rather than leading it.

Too often those of us who have devoted ourselves to building expertise in curriculum development find ourselves holding back and criticising the rapid changes which are being attempted in schools. This is understandable but not excusable. Certainly, our wide perspective on schools and learners makes us wary of the quickly developed, untested innovations which are being introduced. We see too quickly and easily for our own comfort the flaws and the eventualities of many of these proposals. We need, however, to take a more positive leadership stance. We must propose rather than criticize. We must be in the forefront of innovation and change.

It is revealing to consider some possible reasons for our loss of initiative in the current curriculum reform movement. It is from such investigation that we can learn the lessons needed to help us assume the essential leadership. Recollection of the state of the curriculum field and the concern of curriculum people in the early 1940's serves to point to conditions which led to this loss of initiative.

By 1940 the concern for setting goals and interpreting the aims of education into operational guides for teaching had waned. The work of curriculum study groups in the 1920's and 1930's which defined goals in such terms as social functions was widely accepted as the basis for curriculum development. There was little recognition of the need for a continuous redefinition of the purposes of education in American society. The significant effort of Stratemeyer and others in the Horace Mann-Lincoln Institute of School Experimentation at Teachers College following the Second World War to provide direction for curriculum development through a definition of the life situations learners face, though recognized widely, did not generate the widespread efforts at implementation in practice such work deserved. The interest of curriculum people in the late 1940's turned largely to group dynamics. Thus, changes in people became the focus of the curriculum field during this period.

Moving further back in time we can see other possible causes. Roots of the problem may reside in the reaction during the 1920's against an over-emphasis on the sequential arrangement of the content of the academic disciplines as the organizing focus of the curriculum. The changes from this emphasis to an emphasis on individual and group experiences as the focus of curriculum development posed the problem of the place and function of information from the disciplines in the curriculum. How were teachers to choose content and integrate it into the experiences of learners as they pursued problems of immediate concern to them? This question was never satisfactorily answered. Curriculum workers have given too little systematic attention to this problem through the years.

In the late 1940's and early 1950's concern for the dynamics of groups and change in people further de-emphasized academic content as a focus of concern in curriculum development. By the early 1950's strong public reaction against the de-emphasis of academic content became apparent. Progressive Education, a term associated in the minds of many people with a lack of interest in such content, became a term used only by those who wished to deride education.

The launching of Sputnik in 1957 and the consequent fear that the United States was being outdistanced by Russia resulted in the reaction against American education with which we are all familiar. The critics called for an emphasis on academic excellence. There was a scramble to strengthen our programs in mathematics and science. The academicians again focused their attention on an area—the curriculum of the public schools—which they had long neglected. Curriculum specialists, finding themselves bypassed in this period, often became defensive. We thus lost the initiative, and in the decade which has followed curriculum decisions usually have been made by almost everyone except professional curriculum specialists. There is a growing awareness that we cannot continue the haphazard, patchwork approach to curriculum development underway today.

Curriculum specialists must assume a positive leadership role in curriculum designing if there are to emerge unified curriculums focused on the totality of learning experiences. This is not to suggest that the professional curriculum worker must dominate the efforts at curriculum reform or that other groups must desist from their efforts in behalf of better educational experiences for learners. Indeed, it was unfortunate that the academicians withdrew from active involvement in curriculum designing during the early decades of this century.

What is needed today is a truly cooperative effort to bring to bear pertinent areas of knowledge on curriculum designing. A team approach involving curriculum specialists, educational administrators, academicians, behavioral scientists, economists, and others seems to be the answer to the need for fundamental curriculum reform. No one of these groups has the understanding and expertise necessary to build an educational program appropriate for the complex world in which we live today. Ways must be found to bridge the gap which still exists between specialists in these disciplines. Theodore Sizer, Dean of the Graduate School of Education at Harvard University, deplores the gap that exists between academic scholars and professors of education. He says, ". . . there is no more room for such silliness, no more room for the high-handed superiority of the 'subject-matter specialists'. . . or the defensive idiocy of many educationists."[2]

Both Dean Sizer of Harvard and Dean Robert Schaefer of Teachers College look to the schools of education to implement the idea of team approaches to curriculum reform. Dean Schaefer, in a recent message to the Teachers College faculty, stressed the importance of a faculty consisting of individuals committed to curriculum development who would also have specific preparation as scholars in a behavioral science or an academic discipline. These individuals, along with specialists in curriculum designing and implementation, would provide the setting in the university or the school where curriculum reform projects could happily find a home. In speaking to this same idea Dean Sizer says, "Since curriculum development is a long-range continuing process, many of the key men involved must be those whose careers are largely devoted to it. The task is too difficult to leave completely to the hit-and-run professor or the part-time worker. We must develop a new generation of professors of education with the kind of expertise required."[3]

An urgent need is to make explicit and apparent the expertness of the curriculum specialist which qualifies him to provide the leadership essential to curriculum designing. There is very promising activity in this direction among curriculum specialists today. Effort is being made to define the curriculum field—its body of knowledge and areas of expertness. We need to get on with this job.

It is readily apparent that designing the curriculum, like any other design-

2 Theodore R. Sizer, "Reform Movement or Panacea?" *Saturday Review,* June 19, 1965, p. 54.

3 *Ibid.,* p. 54.

ing task, requires the mediation of many elements. These elements involve information regarding learners and learning; understanding of the function of content in the development of knowledge; understanding of the teaching act; and information regarding school organization and group dynamics. The mediation of these elements demands a broad perspective that makes it possible to predict the consequences of decisions that initiate interaction of these elements. Demanded is the ability to predict the results of interaction of learners with content, with other learners, with teachers, and with the physical environment. Certainly, effective curriculum planning requires an understanding of the interaction of cognitive, affective, social, and physical forces in the learning processes proposed. Much more needs to be said and done to define the expertness required of those who would supply leadership in curriculum designing, but at this point it can be said that the *wisdom* involved in the mediation of the design elements is the content of the curriculum field, and this content will define the expertise required.

Whether the mastery of this area of knowledge can be achieved along with another area of expertness chosen from the behavioral sciences or academic disciplines is a matter of conjecture. Certainly, there must be a new generation of professors committed to teamwork in curriculum development.

ATTENTION TO THE POLITICS OF CURRICULUM CHANGE

A significant area of concern is currently receiving the attention of some curriculum specialists. This is the area of curriculum change viewed in the context of the power involved in shaping curriculum policies. This line of endeavor promises to give all of us concerned with the curriculum field a more realistic view of the forces involved in change and thus to identify more sharply the leadership role in curriculum development.

Taking off from the obvious lack of realism on the part of professional curriculum workers regarding the politics of curriculum change, this approach recognizes that *power* and *influence* hold the keys to policy making in education. Professor Dwayne Huebner, writing about the need for political analysis of the situation in curriculum development, has pointed out that educators have for too long lived with an idealized conception of democracy as the means of change. This conception maintains, among other things, that conflicts over educational values are resolved by means of rational argument, scientific research, and intellectual agreement. Those who hold this conception find it difficult to accept the irrationality that often helps to determine social policy and, consequently, have not been able to mobilize emotions and feelings through nondiscursive symbols and even emotive arguments. Huebner writes: "Educators have shied away from power and from politics in their thinking, perhaps because of unfortunate connotations connected with both words, . . . we must accept with Hannah Arendt that politics is one of the great arts of mankind."[4] He says further:

> To keep the phenomena of power, and its quest, in the open and talked about is to make these less frightening. In turn the professional curriculum worker should be less defensive when he wakens one day to find that curricular decisions are being made by someone else, for this fact simply implies that the professional has lost control by default or by not recognizing that power and influence are never permanently institutionalized but always available to the individual who has the know-how to gain it.[5]

Professor Gordon Mackenzie has given considerable attention to the politics of curriculum change. His analysis of determiners of the curriculum and the manner in which the process of change is focused on these determiners serves to clarify the situation which we face in the curriculum today.[6] The system described by Mackenzie includes six determiners of the curriculum: teachers, students, subject matter, methods, materials and facilities, and time. His study points to the necessity of giving attention to all of these as determiners in bringing about significant change. He found, however, that many attempts at change have focused directly on one or more of the determiners, treating *them* as if they were the curriculum change. He cites changes such as team teaching or educational television which have been proposed with little consideration for their impact on the range of curriculum determiners.

Mackenzie's analysis underlines the significance of the cultural context of change. It would be very difficult today to understand the numerous proposals for change without an understanding of the current scene. The powerful influence of feelings of national insecurity and a desire for personal security; rapid advances in science, mathematics, and technology; changes in occupational and living patterns; and pressures toward centralization and national control must be recognized in curriculum innovations.

The power of sanctions administered from various sources within the cultural context must be recognized, according to Mackenzie. Such sanctions

[4] Dwayne Huebner, "Politics and the Curriculum," in A. Harry Passow (Ed.), *Curriculum Crossroads* (New York: Teachers College Press, Teachers College, Columbia University, 1962), pp. 88–98.

[5] Dwayne Huebner, "Politics and Curriculum," *Educational Leadership*, 22, 2, November 1964, p. 117.

[6] Reported in Gordon N. Mackenzie, "Curricular Change: Participants, Power, and Processes," in Matthew B. Miles (Ed.), *Innovation in Education* (New York: Teachers College Press, Teachers College, Columbia University, 1964), pp. 399–424.

as harsh criticisms of the schools, administrators threatened with dismissal, and funds withheld have been used. Fund-granting organizations, for example, have frequently bypassed educators in favor of noneducators who proposed to conduct curriculum studies. Through the use of such sanctions schools and professional educators have been pressured toward greater effort by the demand for quality education, although the direction for doing better often has not been precisely defined by those administering the sanction.

Mackenzie's analysis identifies several classes of participants in the change process. His category of internal participants includes students, teachers, principals, supervisors, superintendents, boards of education, citizens in local communities, state legislatures, state departments of education, and state and federal courts. His category of external participants includes noneducationists, foundations, academicians, business and industry, and the federal government. It is significant to note that Mackenzie found that while internal participants did initiate change the dominant influence came from external participators. Foundations and influential writers and speakers wielded the greatest influence for change among those studied.

The concern for politics and power in curriculum change represents a marked difference from the concern for curriculum change during the 1940's and 1950's. The earlier emphasis lacked the realistic recognition of the need to understand and influence the forces operating in the broader social context. If we can learn to deal with these forces it is possible we may be able to resume the leadership which we have lost for the moment.

ATTENTION TO THE DEVELOPMENT OF CURRICULUM THEORY

One of the urgent needs of the curriculum field today is coherent theory of curriculum development which will serve to give direction to the many decisions which must be made. The current state of confusion in curriculum development stems in large part from a lack of direction and of a sound base for evaluating the many proposals for change which well-conceived theory could provide. There seems to be widespread recognition of such a need but little progress toward the essential theoretical models.

Recognition of the need for curriculum theory is not of recent vintage. Harold Rugg called for a theory of curriculum development in the Twenty-sixth Yearbook of the National Society for the Study of Education published in 1927. He asked for a comprehensive overview of the currents of American life and education, appraisal of the factors in the educational situation, and a recognition of the realities of child growth. He urged a new synthesis—a comprehensive orientation of the relation between the school curriculum and the content of life on the American continent. Such a synthesis could lead, he felt, to a new vision of the direction in which the educational machine should be guided. He warned:

> It is most important that those who are constructing our school curriculum shall maintain an overview of the total situation; lacking that, their orientation will be biased, their emphasis misplaced. There is grave danger that they will continue to commit themselves uncritically to plans and movements—to take up the current modes only to discard them as unthinkingly as they adopted them. Much of the machinery of American education has indeed developed in the past fifty years by just this method.[7]

Professor Rugg's commentary might well have had a publication date in the 1960's, so familiar is the problem he outlines. We have done little to accomplish the goal he so ably defined. The failure by curriculum people to heed such a warning and get on with the essential business of theory development is due to a number of factors.

One such factor might well be the obsession with a means-end model which governed early efforts at curriculum designing and continues into the present time. When the traditional concept of the curriculum as consisting of courses of study gave way to the definition of curriculum as the experiences pupils had under the direction of the school, the focus changed to concern for the means by which the experiences might be directed and improved. Curriculum designing became largely a matter of identifying goals and devising learning activities to realize the goals. Much time, energy, and scholarship have been devoted to goal definition. It has been difficult for curriculum workers to redirect their efforts even though it is apparent that this kind of means-end model does not provide the synthesis necessary today for guiding curriculum designing.

Another factor might well be the hope invested by early curriculum workers in psychology and other disciplines as the sources of theories which would guide curriculum designing. The curriculum field has been, and still is, viewed by many individuals as an applied field. Its purpose, according to these people, is to apply the theories of learning developed by the field of psychology; to apply theories of society and social behavior developed within the field of sociology; or to communicate the moral values of our society which are the concerns of philosophy. This has been a misplaced hope. These fields have not been able to provide the direction desired. Psychology has not yet developed a coherent theory of learning which can serve as a

---

[7] Harold Rugg (Ed.), "Curriculum-Making: Past and Present," *The Foundations and Technique of Curriculum Construction*, Part 1, Twenty-sixth Yearbook of the National Society for the Study of Education (Bloomington, Ill.: Public School Publishing Co., 1926), p. x.

sufficient guide to curriculum designing. Psychologists continue to develop learning models which other psychologists tear apart.

Such activity is repeated in the other disciplines related to education. This is appropriate activity for scholars in a discipline, for it is by this continual seeking for better theoretical models that progress is made. Indeed, theories are not facts to be applied. They are more nearly guesses about past conditions or events which provide the basis for testing new conditions or events. In the process of further investigation and testing new theories develop, and thus new investigations are generated.

This discussion is not to suggest that curriculum development does not require insights from these and other related disciplines. It does, but the problem is how can these insights be applied. It is rather generally recognized now that the application of the results of theoretical formulation and testing in the disciplines related to curriculum designing requires *curriculum* theories that provide the bases for testing these results in schools and classrooms. In the view of those who accept this idea the curriculum field is not an applied field but a field of inquiry in its own right. The theories will be distinctly curriculum theories, and the methods of inquiry will be distinctly curriculum development methods which will generate a body of knowledge unique to the field. Needless to say, much must be done to realize this state of affairs. The curriculum field, however, is a young field, and there is no reason to doubt that its workers will be able to make this necessary definition.

Another factor in the delayed emergence of curriculum theory might well be attributed to the overconcern on the part of curriculum people with the nature of theory itself. Virgil Herrick and Ralph Tyler at the first Conference on Curriculum Theory in 1947 urged that attention be given to describing the nature of the curriculum theory needed. This was done, of course, with the purpose of hastening the development of more adequate curriculum theory. To date, it would seem more attention has been given to the nature of theory than to the formulation of theoretical constructs and their application to problems of curriculum design.

So, while the discussions of the nature of theory itself and the *need* for curriculum theory proceed in many quarters, confusion continues to characterize the state of affairs in curriculum designing. The criteria used for selecting curriculum experiences are many. They come from many sources and operate side-by-side without regard to their consistency or pertinence in specific situations. In some learning experiences the stimulus-response theory of learning governs the choice of methods and materials, and in others the field theory is applied without differentiating the particular relevance of each. Some learning experiences or subjects continue as a part of the curriculum because of tradition; some are introduced because of pressures from the public, and still others, because they, for some vague reason, meet the needs of learners.

There is little direction in organization. Courses representing highly specialized academic areas exist alongside courses representing combinations of the content of several disciplines. Courses that focus on life problems are included with courses that focus on an academic discipline for the discipline's sake. It has been shown that administrative arrangements are made for grouping pupils or setting up teams of teachers without concern for a redefinition of content or teaching methods to make them appropriate to the new organization. Sequences of courses or experiences follow no clear-cut principles. Administrative convenience often dictates the placement of subjects or courses. New experiences or courses are added without careful and thorough consideration of overlapping with what is being taught elsewhere. Taba attributes such confusion in large part to our attempts to apply directly the theories from related disciplines. She says:

> This confusion has many sources, not the least of which is a lack of clarity and outright conflicts in the basic sciences from which education draws its data and guiding principles. Chief among the conflicts are those in the philosophical and psychological theories regarding the nature of the individual, the nature of learning, the goals of our culture, and the individual in that culture. . . . There are disagreements about the functions of the school in our society. Only scattered hints are available about the basic character of the American culture; there are differences about its chief values, and hence, also, about the kind of individual needed in this culture.
>
> When these conflicting ideas are applied to curriculum making, they cease to be mere theoretical details: they acquire pragmatic importance.[8]

There are those in our ranks who are devoting considerable time and attention to this problem. Some of the recent attempts to study the teaching act are moving the field in the desired direction. The attempts of some people to differentiate between the concepts of *curriculum, teaching,* and *instruction* and to develop models of curriculum planning systems and instruction systems which can be analyzed in terms of input and output components offer promising leads. It seems, however, that there must be support for continuing effort on the part of many groups to develop guiding theories. We cannot leave such a crucial area to the scattered efforts of individuals, no matter how competent and dedicated.

---

[8] Hilda Taba, *Curriculum Development Theory and Practice* (New York: Harcourt, Brace and World, 1962), p. 7.

ATTENTION TO THE DEVELOPMENT OF APPROPRIATE METHODS OF CURRICULUM RESEARCH

A notable characteristic of the period is the attention and reverence paid to research. Indeed, this period might well be viewed as the era of the great *re-search*. There are indications that more people have been involved and more money has been spent on educational research during the first five years of this decade than in the entire history of public education in this country. A study of reports of research proposals and research underway reveals, however, too few well-conceived studies of curriculum problems.

Criticisms of recent curriculum research are many and reflect a diversity of concepts regarding needed research. David Elliott and Arthur W. Foshay report the many criticisms of curriculum research in the June 1963 issue of the *Review of Educational Research*. They indicate that some critics have criticized it for the kinds of problems tackled, some for the procedures used, and some for the way in which the results are used. Some critics point to a lack of sophistication in both researchers and those who would employ their findings. Some see a need for emphasis upon more central research questions and problems and some a need for firmer theoretical grounding for research.

In the same issue of the *Review of Educational Research,* James B. Mac-donald and James D. Raths point to the problems faced by curriculum researchers in attempting to use research models taken from other fields of inquiry. Along with other individuals, they raise the question of the appropriateness of these borrowed models for studying the kinds of questions of concern in curriculum development. The need suggested here is for models of research that will allow study of new methods of instruction, content, instructional materials, administrative arrangements, and the setting for learning. There is need for research that will allow us to study learning situations whole, without the fragmentation involved when we employ research models borrowed from psychology or the physical sciences. Just as the social sciences have found it necessary to develop new research approaches and new concepts of variable control, so must we in the curriculum field develop types of research appropriate to our field of inquiry.

To urge a search for new research models is not to suggest less rigor in design and execution nor less concern for validity in research findings. It is, rather, to recognize the impracticality of research techniques that so limit the type of questions which can be researched as to render research of little consequence in curriculum designing.

It will not be easy to break through the conceptions of respectability which have grown up around traditional research techniques. At one point action research was viewed as a promising model for curriculum research. Traditional researchers viewed it with alarm because it offered few of the traditional controls. As a result, the potential within the model has never been fully tested. Somehow the search for new and promising designs must be systematized. The answer may lie in systematic comparative studies of different research designs to develop and test those appropriate to curriculum inquiry. It is possible that this approach would serve to allay the fears of those who find it difficult to accept research designs which do not follow the traditional models.

The urgent need for sounder bases for making decisions in the curriculum field demands attention to fundamental study and research on the part of great numbers of curriculum specialists. The need to evaluate the many proposals for innovation and the need to develop new curriculum sequences and organizational models call for a widespread cooperative effort on the part of universities and public school systems. The concept of university professors as creators of knowledge through research and school people as implementers of this knowledge in practice has not been effective in producing the coherent curriculum so needed in American schools. Both of these groups must view the task of developing, implementing, and evaluating curriculum practices as a single job requiring their individual talents.

What is needed is the development of new practices under carefully conceived experimental conditions followed by rigorous testing and evaluation in a variety of schools and communities. Each of these steps requires the cooperative effort of both public school and university personnel. Experimental situations, though controlled in many respects, must approximate as far as possible certain of the realities of the situations into which the practices will eventually find their way. Indeed, only in this way can we lay an adequate groundwork for systematic testing in other situations. Team effort will make possible this reality at both the experimental and testing stages.

Such a plan has been employed by the federal government in its program of agricultural experimentation and testing. Regional experimental farms have developed new practices which are studied very carefully by farmers of the region. At an appropriate point the practices then are tested on a number of farms under a variety of conditions. The new proposal of the U. S. Office of Education for the development of regional laboratories for developing and testing educational practices would appear to be following somewhat this same pattern. This is an effort that can be highly productive of effective curriculum development if supported by public schools and universities of the regions. These laboratories alone will not accomplish the job which needs to be done. There will need to be widespread cooperation among individual school systems and schools of education to make needed progress.

SUMMARY

The major problem in curriculum reform today is the lack of a coherent structure for initiating and evaluating innovation. Many of the current proposals for change do not fit together, and too few people are concerned with their total impact on learners. Moreover, the piecemeal nature of such curriculum innovation is freezing many aspects of school organization which are in serious need of examination and reform. The basic need is for curriculum theory which will provide the base for developing up-to-date curriculums that do fit together.

Although the problems are many, there has never before existed the great opportunity for real progress in curriculum development inherent in the current scene. There is widespread public interest in education. There is an increasing recognition of the need for adequate support of education if it is to fulfill the role it can play in our nation's development. There is a kind of readiness for change which is all pervasive. Leadership is needed in harnessing this potential—leadership that recognizes the need for continuous redefinition of curriculum to meet changing needs and concepts of education.

THE GIFTED AND
THE DISADVANTAGED:
SOME CURRICULUM INSIGHTS

A. HARRY PASSOW

SOME FIFTEEN YEARS have now elapsed since the beginning of what some call the "third wave of interest in the gifted and the talented." In the early 1950's, educators once again asked if we were short-changing the gifted and whether our schools were, as the Educational Policies Commission put it, up to "the weighty task of giving life to the great ideal of educational opportunity for the varied children of a heterogeneous people." Critical shortages in trained manpower combined with the reappraisal of American education to set the stage for the current look at the adequacy of educational provisions for able youngsters. While the event of Sputnik accelerated (perhaps *panicked* is a better adjective) and, in a sense, legitimized the intensified search for talent, the schools and the public had been prepared already. Programs multiplied factorially; experimentation and research increased sharply. In the intervening years, some innovations have become more or less institutionalized while practices which were sharply debated a decade ago are accepted with little question today.

. In 1954, shortly after the Horace Mann-Lincoln Institute's Talented Youth Project was initiated, Abraham Tannenbaum and I mailed letters to more than one hundred school systems that Paul Witty had named in a 1941 NEA publication on programs for the gifted. We asked each superintendent in Witty's survey whether the program was still in operation, what modifications had taken place, and whether any evaluative reports or other materials were available. Independently, Brandwein had conducted a simi-

---

A. HARRY PASSOW is Professor of Education at Teachers College, Columbia University.

lar though less systematic survey of science programs for gifted students. Due to the informal nature of both surveys, neither has ever been reported in the literature. Both underscored the ephemeral nature of educational programs, especially those which seem to depend on the continuing concern of a single individual. Provisions for the gifted had languished during the 1940's. Programs then were essentially administrative (e.g., ability grouping, grade skipping, and rapid promotion) with little in the way of significant curriculum adaptations. Evaluation was minimal, consisting of comparisons of achievement by "homogeneous" and "heterogeneous" groups; of academic attainment through acceleration by rapid promotion; and of pupil, parent, and teacher testimony about a particular program.

I would like to think that were we to replicate our survey of programs for the gifted now the findings would be somewhat different. It is true that we jump from one bandwagon to another, but some evidence can be mustered to suggest that today's programs for the gifted, at least the instructional variety, are more thoughtfully conceived and more stable than earlier programs. We still do not have an acceptable theory of talent development nor are the dimensions of an adequate curriculum for the gifted as clear as they might be.

"Enrichment" is the panacea in prescriptions for teaching the gifted. Our definition and understanding of enrichment still leave much to be desired. Consequently, when we discuss enrichment programs for the gifted child, the observation is inevitably made: "But a rich curriculum is what we want for *all* children." We nod our agreement and add that individual differences endow richness with different meanings. Differentiated experiences are called for if richness is to be realized. *Adequacy* and *appropriateness* are terms used with more meaning than "richness."

In the early fifties, we talked about a broadened definition of talent to include unusual performance in any socially valuable area, but our provisions aimed essentially at the academically able child. We have come since to understand that giftedness is multifaceted. The narrow definition of giftedness has been altered even as the conceptions of nature of intelligence have changed. Guilford's model of the structure of intellect consisting of relatively discrete though related aspects of intellectual functioning triggered the development of techniques which aimed at assessing abilities other than those appraised by conventional measures of intelligence. Getzels and Jackson, in applying Guilford's work directly to the school setting, called for a broader definition of giftedness:

> Once we set a precedent by allowing an exception to the practice of labeling only high IQ children as "gifted," the possibility of expanding the concept to include other potentially productive groups becomes a

genuine challenge to both educators and research workers. The not inconsiderable dangers inherent in the possibility of expanding the concept to a point where it becomes meaningless seem to us to be compensated by the possibility of increasing the effectiveness of our education for *all* children.[1]

The development and application of measures of divergent thinking have spread out in the past few years. The conception of giftedness has been expanded to include various kinds of intellectual functioning. Guilford saw implications for education for his ideas concerning the components of intelligence which went far beyond psychological testing. He suggested fundamental transformations of our conceptions of the learner and the learning process.

> If education has the general objective of developing the intellects of students, it can be suggested that each intellectual factor provides a particular goal at which to aim. Defined by a certain combination of content, operation, and product, each goal ability then calls for certain kinds of practice in order to achieve improvement in it. This implies choice of curriculum and the choice or invention of teaching methods that will most likely accomplish the desired results.[2]

The concern with creativity, divergent thinking, and productive behavior as elements of instructional programs tends still to be more plea than program. DeMille suggests two different paths for introducing more creativity into curricula:

> Creativity can be thought of as a new sort of subject matter or skill that is to be imparted by means of language, numbers, graphic and musical activities, dramatics, etc. Or, the existing curriculum can be thought of as the essential core, and an effort can be made to teach it in a better way by bringing out the creativity implicit in it. The curriculum can be a vehicle for creativity or creativity can enhance the curriculum.[3]

While there have been some inquiries into the merits of grouping youngsters on the basis of "creativity scores," they have been relatively few. Instead, it seems to me that we have concerned ourselves with instructional questions, such as whether some content areas have greater possibilities for nurturing the development of creative abilities, whether the creative process can be considered apart from or unrelated to content areas, and whether certain intellectual operations are precursors for productive behavior in the educational setting.

[1] J. W. Getzels and P. W. Jackson, "The Meaning of 'Giftedness'—An Examination of an Expanding Concept," *Phi Delta Kappan*, 40, 1958, pp. 75–77.

[2] J. P. Guilford, "Three Faces of Intellect," *American Psychologist*, 14, 1959, p. 479.

[3] R. DeMille, "The Creativity Boom," *Teachers College Record*, 65, 1963, p. 205.

Taba suggests that curriculum planning for an orderly development of creativity requires a careful analysis of content organization as well as determination of sequence of learning experiences. She says:

> One must analyze the nature of the subjects to determine which ideas and concepts are basic and which details most economically provoke these ideas. Both the content ideas and the mental operations for dealing with them must be organized in a cumulative hierarchy of ascending abstractness and complexity in order to demand a greater range of association, more precise differentiation, a higher level of abstraction, and a wider scope of transfer and application.[4]

Thus, the expanded notions of giftedness and its many faceted nature have spurred the development of appropriate assessment procedures which might supplement conventional techniques. But, in addition, they have resulted in the more systematic analysis of curriculum content and methodology toward the end of developing more of the general and specific intellectual skills which comprise giftedness.

The concern with creativity and its nurture is, of course, only a piece of the total concern with the development of giftedness. In the more traditional subject areas, such as mathematics and science, new curriculum proposals have poured forth since the mid-1950's. The Advanced Placement Program (now reaching more than thirty thousand students) and the BSCS Biology Study for Gifted Students are two programs aimed at the academically talented student. Few of the others claim to be directed specifically at the intellectually gifted students, but, by dealing with content and processes calling for higher abstract and conceptual levels, many of the newer curricula seem especially appropriate for the more able student. However, there is little question that in the attempt to become discipline-centered, to stress intuitive thinking, to emphasize the abstract and the conceptual rather than the informational, to build greater depth and breadth of experience, these newer curriculum proposals affect the intellectually gifted children rather directly.

Over the years, as we have come to recognize that administrative arrangements per se, without differentiation in content, method, and instructional resources, make little difference, we have shifted attention to curriculum content—scope, sequence, and structure. We have had curriculum changes for the gifted that might be characterized as vertical changes—i.e., moving content down so that youngsters have contact with particular material at an earlier age or in less time than is normal; horizontal changes,—i.e., study in greater depth and breadth than is usual; reorganizational kinds of change—

---

[4] Hilda Taba, "Opportunities for Creativity in Education for Exceptional Children," *Exceptional Children*, 29, 1963, p. 256.

i.e., the redesigning and redefinition of the curriculum content itself; or, change through augmentation—i.e., the introduction of courses or units which have not been part of the usual academic curriculum, such as the Mathematics of Science, Integration of the Arts, and Biology of Space Exploration. Elements of anthropology, biophysics, sociology, social psychology, and geopolitics have found their way into elementary and secondary school curricula for gifted children. Seminars on standard and esoteric topics, as well as flexible schedules, have become standard in many school programs. What part of the "curriculum revolution" of the past dozen years is due to concern with the gifted is difficult to assess, but there is little question that this concern has played a significant role.

Of course, all of the provisions and adaptations above have not resulted in the fullest development of all individual potential talents. The causes of underachievement still remain unclear, especially when one attempts to explain the discrepancy between prediction and attainment of an individual youngster. But here, again, the interest in these discrepancies have resulted in analyses of intellectual and non-intellectual determinants of learning and in efforts to programmatically close the gap between prediction and attainment.

Our experiences with groups of children identified as gifted have made apparent that the range of individual differences is extremely broad. There are individuals who are generally gifted, while others are outstanding in a single area. Some gifted individuals are just slightly better than average while others are so unusual as to be rare. Some individuals show their abilities very early and others are "late bloomers." That giftedness is a complex phenomenon is obvious. Merely identifying and labeling a child as gifted will not insure development of his talents. What seems to be happening is that we are now testing McClelland's hypothesis that "talent potential may be fairly widespread, a characteristic which can be transformed into actually talented performance by various sorts of the right kinds of education."[5] The present concern for the education of the disadvantaged had at least part of its origin in the fact that children from depressed areas—those from low-income, ethnic and racial minority backgrounds—probably represent the largest reservoir of undeveloped potential.

The New York City Demonstration Guidance Project, begun in December 1956, tested the hypothesis that, given guidance, remedial help, and supplemental experiences, youngsters from culturally deprived groups would exhibit greater potential than they normally do. Initially, pupils who showed the greatest academic potential at Junior High School 43 in Man-

[5] D. C. McClelland, "Issues in the Identification of Talent," in McClelland et al., *Talent and Society* (Princeton: Van Nostrand, 1958), p. 25.

hattan were involved in the six-year project, even though their scores were far below the usual cut-off point. The results were sufficiently promising to warrant the Higher Horizons Program. This project did not include what were apparently the key elements of the Demonstration Guidance Project so that the consequences were far less promising. Other programs, spurred first by private foundations and more recently by governmental support, have emerged since. The hope that educational experiences will help increase the talent reservoir has been expressed by the Conservation of Human Resources Project's observation:

> Superior performance in any society is limited by the number of individuals with a high order of intelligence but in our society the number of such individuals could be substantially increased through improving the opportunities for members of the lower socio-economic classes to become interested in and to acquire a good education.[6]

As the schools have become centrally involved in the war on poverty and the civil rights struggle, they have really been asked to reaffirm their traditional function of providing equal educational opportunities for all. Some of the early programs for disadvantaged youth focused as much on the conative-affective development of disadvantaged youth as on their cognitive growth. For instance, the Dillard Pre-Freshman Program is one example of a college-based program which, with many variations, aims at bringing disadvantaged individuals into an environment designed as much to affect their motivation as to contribute to intellectual growth.

The President's Panel on Educational Research and Development has flatly declared that "by all known criteria, the majority of urban and rural slum schools are failures."[7] The panel supported its charge by citing the severe scholastic retardation which steadily worsens as children grow older; the dropout rate which exceeds 50 per cent, fewer than 5 per cent going on to some form of higher education; and a general picture of adolescents leaving school "ill-prepared to lead a satisfying, useful life or to participate successfully in the community."[8] Significantly, the panel expressed the conviction that, while additional funds for more classrooms and improved teacher-pupil ratios would certainly help, more important are programs of curriculum development and teacher education. Spurred by legislation and federal funds as well as by pricked consciences, educators have become concerned with the disadvantaged, following some of the same patterns we did

[6] D. W. Bray, *Issues in the Study of Talent* (New York: Columbia University Press, 1954), p. 16.

[7] Panel in Research and Development, *Innovation and Experiment in Education* (Washington, D.C.: United States Government Printing Office, 1964), p. 30.

[8] *Ibid.*

with the gifted a dozen years ago. There still is debate about an acceptable label and definition, but operationally, the disadvantaged population is considered to include the economically impoverished, racial-ethnic minority groups with severe problems of academic retardation. The programs initiated fall into a limited number of general patterns, including:

1. Pre-school and early childhood programs aimed at compensating for early experiential deficits, especially those of language and cognitive development.

2. Reassessment and development of curriculum content to facilitate acculturation in an urbanized, technological society.

3. Remedial programs in the basic skill areas.

4. Enrichment projects to overcome cultural impoverishment, enhance motivation, and "widen the horizons" of pupils from depressed areas.

5. Special guidance programs to extend counseling and therapy services to disadvantaged pupils and their parents. Parent education—which interprets the educational needs and potential of disadvantaged children to their parents—is gaining significance as a guidance function.

6. Individual and small-group tutoring programs with professionals, paraprofessionals and volunteers of all kinds to enhance the individual's self concept as well as provide him with personal remedial assistance.

7. Lengthening of school day and year and extension of activities into the community and neighborhood.

8. Pre-service and in-service teacher training to deepen teachers' understanding of the life styles and growth patterns of children from depressed areas. Also, to test and to improve teaching strategies and methods which might work with low-income children.

9. Development of materials to involve the disadvantaged child, to extend his cognitive development, and to provide needed remedial assistance.

10. Work-study and continuation programs now involve work exploration, on-the-job training, and subsidized work experience. Continuing education, especially for the sixteen to twenty-one-year-olds, has resulted in new kinds of school programs.

11. Additional staff are being assigned to schools in depressed areas and staff utilization patterns are being adapted. As many as a dozen "special service personnel" are used to augment regular faculty positions in schools with disadvantaged pupils.

We now face the danger that, just as with the planning for the gifted, pressures to initiate programs will result in creating structures with form but without substance. For instance, pre-school programs are springing up everywhere with all too little pre-planning being given to the development of an adequate curriculum for the disadvantaged groups to be served. (Incidentally, when one remembers the debates which raged over early admission to kindergarten for bright children, the headlong rush to pre-school programs is even more interesting.) And yet, educators could utilize the rich research literature as a basis for understanding the general characteristics of the disadvantaged, supplement these with diagnostic techniques for a specific group, and construct a curriculum which would provide a series of sequentially ordered activities in the specific areas of compensatory need of this population. These activities could then be balanced with the more general developmental experiences appropriate for all children. An adequate pre-school program for disadvantaged children must be basically compensatory, in the sense of overcoming specific experiential and cognitive deficits.

At the Institute of Developmental Studies, for example, the emphasis has been on the "role of specific social attributes and experiences in the development of language and verbal behavior, of concept formation and organization, of visual and auditory discrimination, of general environmental orientation, and of self-concepts and motivation; and of all this to school performance."[9] The Institute staff has attempted to evolve curriculum, techniques, and materials in language, math, science, reading skills, and concept formation—all of which comprise what Deutsch calls a "therapeutic curriculum." Whatever its shortcomings, it does represent an attempt to diagnose the particular needs of a specific school population and to evolve a curriculum aimed at reversing the effects of social deprivation. Similarly, Bereiter and his associates at the University of Illinois are testing an unusual pre-school curriculum with fifteen culturally deprived children. Bereiter's curriculum is academically oriented, using direct instruction that focuses upon the basic information processes that are necessary for thinking with the content areas of basic language training, reading, and arithmetic. His approach involves:

> . . . (1) analysis of the formal characteristics of language, reading and arithmetic that are relevant to young culturally deprived children, (2) translating these into instructional goals, (3) discovering feasible means of carrying on direct instruction with young culturally deprived children, (4) determining how much of what we would like to teach actually can be taught to children of this kind, and (5) assessing the rate of learning which can be achieved.[10]

[9] Martin Deutsch, "Facilitating Development in the Pre-school Child: Social and Psychological Perspective," *Merrill-Palmer Quarterly*, 10, 1964, p. 258.

[10] C. Bereiter et al., "An Academically Oriented Preschool for Culturally Deprived Children," unpublished paper, University of Illinois, 1965.

While Bereiter's approach probably horrifies a good many nursery and pre-school people, the procedure he is following for selecting and organizing educational experiences is based upon an analysis of the nature of the learner and of knowledge. Finally, he is subjecting his premises to a rigorous and systematic test.

What is required for curriculum development with the disadvantaged is an understanding of the particular patterning of intellectual and cognitive abilities of specific children and of strategies which might be employed to teach directly certain skills, attitudes, and behavior and the selection of content aimed at providing what Hunt calls the "proper match" between the child's developmental level and materials and activities provided. As with the gifted, the programs are patchworks. Few programs for the disadvantaged follow an articulated, integrated approach. Too frequently some remedial services are scheduled, a guidance counselor is added, a taste of work experience is provided, or more Negroes are included in the illustrations of a basal reader series.

Education in the inner-city school has dimensions which are far less crucial with more advantaged children in more favored schools. The disadvantaged learner must obtain an education which will insure development of his potential. It must heighten his ego development and yield a positive self image, preparing him for taking his place in the mainstream of society as a parent, a citizen, and a worker. A curriculum for the disadvantaged must deal with such diverse problems as "reversing the spiral of futility"—the deep-seated belief that the American dream is not for the disadvantaged but for others and that one really cannot break out of the world of the ghetto, poverty, and discrimination; overcoming a deprecatory self image; compensating for cognitive deficiencies which have stemmed from limited environmental stimulation and experiences; developing the learning-how-to-learn skill; and building the kind of general education which will nurture individual potential in a population where it has remained essentially dormant.

What are some of the insights we have gained over the past dozen years or so, as we have developed programs for the gifted and for the disadvantaged? These observations seem relevant:

1. The most important lesson is to attend to the curriculum—content, methods, resources, learning environment—as the focus of our planning efforts. Let us stop expecting that administrative arrangements per se will bring about desired instructional improvement.
2. Programs which have been conceived as part of an integrated, articulated, sequential plan are more likely to have a sustained educational

impact than the patchwork tinkering that is more typical of many school programs.

3. Focusing on the diverse populations whom we label *gifted* or *disadvantaged* can provide us with the kinds of diagnostic and analytic insights which force consideration of the individual needs of students and of differentiation of instruction required. By considering the range of individual differences which the teacher confronts in populations which are either gifted or disadvantaged, we recognize the real limitations in techniques and know-how of provisions for individual differences. To the extent that we really confront this perennial problem of individualizing instruction, essentially because our traditional techniques have failed, we will contribute significantly to upgrading the instructional process. John Hersey reminded us that, "Our uncertainty about exactly how to develop talent is only one part of the greatest unsolved problem in American education—the problem of how to help every child realize his maximum potential; the problem, in the lingo of the trade, of individual differences."[11]

4. By analyzing curriculum content to clarify what it is we want learned and by developing better strategies for arranging conditions for these learnings to occur, the likelihood is that we will acquire the insights which can lead to instructional upgrading for all. There is some evidence to indicate that there is considerable spill-over from various programs for the gifted.

5. In attending to the consequences of self-esteem, aspirations for achievement, and general personality adjustment of living in an urban society, curriculum workers could make a major breakthrough for the acculturation process in the urban setting. While the curriculum worker rarely participates in policy decisions regarding desegregation and racial balance, for instance, he can be invaluable by providing the kind of environment and program which lead to integration within the classroom, school, and community. Perhaps by attending to curriculum matters we can avoid some of the crisis planning we seem to face continually.

Finally, the curriculum worker should have learned that it does little good to sit around and complain about the fact that leadership in program development has been "usurped" by the subject matter specialist, the social psychologist, the politicians. The crucial educational needs of our time are

---

[11] John Hersey, "Wanted: a Larger Frame of Reference," in Nelson B. Henry (Ed.), *Education for the Gifted,* Part II, Fifty-seventh Yearbook of the National Society for the Study of Education (Chicago: Chicago University Press, 1958), p. 5.

patently clear, just as they were a decade or so ago. Whether we are focusing on the gifted or the disadvantaged the prime need is to capitalize on the insights and on teaching strategies and content adaptations that will indeed provide adequately for the vast range of individual differences as such. Without minimizing the other factors which effect educational programs, I would point out that, just as the curriculum worker was slow in recognizing the significance of the challenge and the promise in developing appropriate educational provisions for the gifted, he may now miss the intrinsic benefits presented by our national concern for the disadvantaged. He may undertake the expedient, the superficial, the ephemeral rather than lending his expertise to others who have specialized skills to contribute in the development of the kinds of programs which will enrich our talent reservoirs.

The challenge to the curriculum worker is to assimilate what we have learned from our experience with the gifted and apply it to provisions for the disadvantaged in such a fashion that equal educational opportunity for *all* becomes more of a reality.

THE PERSON
IN THE CURRICULUM

James B. Macdonald

WHAT IS SAID HERE is in the form of a value commitment. This is so simply because the *person* has been put into a curriculum context. This implies that we will *do* something *with, for,* or *to* the person—and any human action is a resolution of thought and feeling into doing by way of a value commitment.

Some persons may wish to discount what will be said because it is labeled a value position. This is certainly appropriate and understandable. Yet we cannot escape values if we are to act at all, and a convenient retreat to "social reality," such as one may witness in the technological talk of educators, does not remove the value problem.

Thus, if we wish to talk about teaching machines and other wondrous schemes, and justify their use by the social reality of progress, we only submerge the inherent value context of the phenomena. The decision to use technology in the schools embodies a value commitment of the first order.

Anything we do in schools can be seen as having both a truth value, i.e., being true or false, and having a moral value, i.e., being right or wrong. Each activity we instigate can be looked at in terms of empirical or analytical truth or falsity, and in terms of the moral dimension of right or wrong.

What we do that is true or false can be verified in terms of some means–ends scheme of analysis, some evaluated objective. What we do that is right or wrong does not depend upon its consequence but upon its quality in the doing of it. Thus, it is completely possible to do a truthful thing—

JAMES B. MACDONALD is Professor of Education at the University of Wisconsin at Madison.

38

for example, make learning more efficient—and at the same time do a wrong thing, that is, something that has an immoral quality to it. It should be obvious that we should strive whenever possible to do things that are both true and right in curriculum activity.

The value commitment proposed here is the dominant concern for what is right. Thus, it is suggested that an act cannot be both right and true at the beginning, but must be a true act made as moral as possible; or, a right act made as true as possible.

Reid and Znaniecki both reflect this dilemma of the necessity of a dominant value in other different discipline contexts. Reid, an English philosopher, says, "The order we give to the values must depend, it would seem, upon commitment to some dominating belief."[1] Znaniecki, a sociologist, describes human action as a series of concrete acts which are built around a central dominant value theme.[2] Thus, both reflect the necessity of ordering activity by some dominant value commitment.

The dominant value proposed here is a moral value and the concept of a person is a moral concept. Education, and more particularly schooling, is thus a moral enterprise because we create a contrived environment, called "curriculum and instruction," and we attempt to influence persons in this environment. We assume the responsibility for the influencing of persons in the directions of our curriculum specifications, and this is essentially a moral act.

THE DISTINCTION BETWEEN THE INDIVIDUAL AND THE PERSON

The term, *individual,* is for the most part a psychological metaphor. It is related to the differences in development, personality, and learning we stress in curriculum and instruction. For example, we say that individuals develop at different rates; that their personalities are formed by their unique past experiences; that they learn in different styles and at different rates. There is no single empirical set of facts relevant to education that is more firmly established than the uniqueness of the individual. We know this by our assessment of abilities, traits, life histories, and performances in the classroom setting.

The *person,* however, in contrast to the individual, is not prized for his uniqueness. His uniqueness is simply a fact known to us through the efforts of biological and psychological inquiry. The person is valued because

[1] L. A. Reid, *Philosophy and Education,* (New York: Random House, 1962).
[2] Florian Znaniecki, *Cultural Sciences: Their Origin and Development* (Urbana: University of Illinois Press, 1952).

of what he shares in common with all other persons: the human condition. Each person strives to create meaning out of his existence in the world, and attempts to gain freedom from crippling fear, anxiety, and guilt. Each person shares the common fate of his mortality and possesses the potential for expressing joy, awe, and wonder. The awareness that all we know with certainty is that *we* are *here,* and that there are *others like us,* characterizes the human condition and makes the person of value. Thus, it is not the uniqueness of the individual in terms of his personal perceptions, idiosyncratic needs, desires, and motives that makes him of value; it is his common human status.

To treat persons as individuals (in the psychological sense) is in essence to treat them as objects for our study and control. The *person* is a *subject* (in contrast to an object) and possesses his own unity. Mounier expresses this contrast well when he says:

> If I treat another person as though he were not present, or as a repository of information for my use, an instrument at my disposal; or when I set him down in a list without right of appeal—in such a case I am behaving towards him as though he were an object, which means in effect, despairing of him. But if I treat him as a subject, as a presence —which is to recognize that I am unable to classify him, that he is inexhaustible, filled with hopes upon which he alone can act—that is to give him credit. To despair of anyone is to make him desperate: whereas the credit that generosity extends regenerates his own confidence.[3]

Contrast this for a moment with the common school practices of grouping, evaluating, and other forms of manipulation done for the sake of the "individual," and some of the problems of dropouts, failures, and those bored in our schools, and the distinction will become clear.

THE CURRICULUM

We see the person in the schools in the context of what we call the curriculum. The meaning of this term is not very precise, and there is considerable dispute and confusion among the meanings of such concepts as curriculum, instruction, teaching, and learning.[4] Let it suffice, for purposes here, to say that we are focused upon the contrived environment and its directed influence upon the person in the schools.

[3] E. Mounier, *Personalism,* translated by Philip Mairet (London: Routledge and Kegan Paul, 1952), p. 23.

[4] See J. B. Macdonald, "Educational Models for Instruction," in J. B. Macdonald and Robert Leeper (Eds.), *Theories of Instruction,* Report of tenth annual Research Institute of the Association of Supervision and Curriculum Development (Washington, D.C., ASCD, 1965), for a discussion of these distinctions.

The curriculum is contrived in the sense that it is neither the immediate "real" world of the student, nor is it the "real" world of the social creators of the meanings, symbols, and skills which make up the substance of curriculum. Further, this environment is characterized by the use of social influence upon the person through the selective criteria used and the social agents (primarily the teachers) in the situation. Thus, in the planning we include and exclude aspects of the larger world by what we see as adequate criteria, and in the classroom context we attempt to influence students toward agreed-upon ways of encountering this contrived environment.

The manner by which we select and influence has come to be characterized as curriculum decision making. Curriculum decisions have been described and discussed by many curriculum scholars.

There are two basic modes of dealing with curriculum decisions. These modes are related to the values of truth and goodness mentioned previously. Within these basic modes there are undoubtedly many possibilities of variation.

Curriculum decision models whose dominant modes are truth-seeking are means-end schema. The decisions made are oriented toward producing the best results in the most efficient manner. The Tyler[5] model is characteristic of this approach. First, it is necessary to identify objectives. These objectives are stated in terms of expected behavioral outcomes. Next, learning experiences are selected and fitted, or organized, in scope and sequence patterns. The final step is the evaluation of outcomes and the renewal of the cycle. When the decisions made in this cycle are sensible and productive, objectives are realized in behavioral terms, and it can be said that we know how to (in a truth-value framework) influence students effectively in our curriculum environment. This is an ideal model for decision making which focuses upon the individual as a psychological entity in schools.

This is, however, precisely the reason why this model is not appropriate for persons. It assumes the psychological knowledge of the individual in relation to his objective performances in the classroom. In so doing it violates the integrity of the person by segmenting his behavior and manipulating him for an end beyond his immediate experiencing in the curriculum.

The second mode of curriculum decision making is focused upon the goodness or rightness of the decisions made in relation to the person. Its beginning point is what is right, *now*, for the person. The learning experience itself must have inherent worth for the person, not in terms of some eventual behavior change, but in terms of its moral quality in the present.

[5] Ralph Tyler, *Basic Principles of Curriculum and Instruction*, Syllabus for Education 360 (Chicago: University of Chicago Press, 1950).

There is no escape from the curriculum dimensions of a contrived environment and influence in our society as long as the schools maintain anything resembling their present form, but a curriculum decision making pattern can be constructed which maximizes the creation of conditions for growth of the person, and it is one possible conception of this kind of curriculum that I would like to turn to now.

A PERSON-ORIENTED CURRICULUM

Our cultural heritage is the substance of our curriculum, whether embodied in symbols set down in material form or carried in the feelings, attitudes, and skills of its members. Further, each person in society must by necessity encounter and be developed within the context of the socialization process. Thus, it is a tempting and seductive rational step to decide that the culture should be divided into logically meaningful segments and the person placed into a social setting whereby the socialization process of our schools operates to achieve the internalizing of the cultural content. Were this the only alternative available schools would be totally characterized by what Mumford[6] calls (in a cultural context) merely *standardization* and *reproduction*.

Man's dilemma, however, arises in the fact that he makes choices and he responds personally to his environment. It is not the fact that he can be conditioned in the socialization process that is in dispute; it is, in contrast, the potentiality for becoming more than his conditions by making choices and having responsibility to the world that poses the dilemma. Or to put it another way, as Reid has:

> It is not just the *fact* of "personality" which is important (and it is important) as (it is) the *values* which the expanding growth of personality can make real. It is through an idea, or an ideal, of what the personality can be, and *ought* to be, that we judge the relative value and importance of various values . . .[7]

Thus, a person-oriented curriculum would by necessity allow for choice and freedom within the context of the school. But freedom and choice are found within boundaries. The limits of freedom are the necessities for maintaining the integrity of other persons; and the meaning of choice is cast in the availability and knowledge of viable alternatives. Thus, the

---

[6] Lewis Mumford, *Art and Technics*, (New York: Columbia University Press, 1962).

[7] Reid, *op.cit.*, p. 64.

school has the responsibility for providing order in interpersonal relationships and acquainting the student with his potential for choice.

The concern for freedom has too often been twisted by the psychological concept of permissiveness. It has carried the connotation of primarily free physical movement and social divergence. It is not that these connotations are necessarily inappropriate in the larger society, but in the school, as the contrived environment of the curriculum, freedom must most appropriately mean freedom of the rational man, the freedom to pursue knowledge with commitment; or, the unimpeded process of building patterns of personal knowledge systems out of the knowledge "stuff" of our world. Thus, the moral expression of the mature role, in the context of the school, is creating the social, physical, and cultural conditions necessary for freedom to flourish.

Choice is meaningless without viable alternatives. The school, again, must define "viable" in terms of the accumulated knowledge and wisdom of mankind. Its task is not to transmit this knowledge, per se, but to provide the awareness of alternatives with which choice may operate creatively in every man's struggle for personal meaning.

The creation of maximal conditions for the person would appear to follow readily from the analogy of culture in a biological-science sense. Thus, the criteria for selecting a contrived environment are conditions for culturing, rather than for being cultured.

The person, by analogy to biological organisms, is assumed to have some innate design and direction in his growth which under the proper conditions, let us say analogous to temperature, light, moisture, nutrients, and soil or saline solution, emerges into being. Such assertions as Maslow's "self-actualization"[8] are psychophilosophical corollaries of this position.

In the case of the person, however, in contrast to bacteria in a culture dish, the human need to do what Langer calls "transform reality symbolically"[9] adds the dimension of the struggle of each person to make order, pattern, and meaning out of existence, and, hence, the necessity for choice and the freedom of choice in order that he may realize himself in his world. These are the conditions necessary to transcend one's own culture and socialization process in order to become a person.

---

[8] Abraham H. Maslow, "Some Basic Propositions of a Growth and Self-Actualizing Psychology," in Arthur W. Combs (Ed.), *Perceiving, Behaving, Becoming*, Yearbook of the Association for Supervision and Curriculum Development (Washington, D.C.: the Association, 1962).

[9] Suzanne Langer, *Philosophy in a New Key* (Cambridge: Harvard University Press, 1957).

CONDITIONS FOR CULTURING PERSONS

The curriculum at its broadest and from any value position must be concerned with the conditions of cultural data, the social conditions within the school, and the physical conditions.

The problem of cultural data or subject matter in the schools is not that it is separate but that it is *separated*, and specifically that it is separated in itself and from the person. In its present, packaged form it is segmented, highly specialized, and unrelated by subjects and unrelated to persons. If the purpose and function of knowledge is to improve the human condition, then the present unrelated form of knowledge cannot help but be reflected in unrelatedness in human experience.

The crucial subject-matter problems in selecting a curriculum and influencing persons within this environment are the problems of relating one aspect of culture to another and relating subject matter to the personal knowledge of the student. The present curriculum activity which updates or reconceptualizes the separate structures of culture is highly desirable, but it is essentially a necessary "given" for struggling with the central issues, the problems of relationship.

Although the two problems of relationship are from one perspective a single issue, it may be useful to separate them into the planning and operating phases of the curriculum. The relationships between subjects fall more readily into the planning phases, and the relating of subject matter to persons falls in the operational or instructional activity.

The problem of planning for the relatedness of knowledge is a vastly difficult task. Few if any persons have the breadth of understanding and wisdom to venture to approach this task with anything but uncertainty. Programs of general education have been discussed for decades with little resolution. The core curriculum was predicated upon this hope; yet we have not resolved this approach to our satisfaction. A modest opinion, suggested by the writings of Earl Johnson[10] may be helpful, however.

At the very least our planning could recognize the unity of knowledge skills. Men dig for facts because they are curious; they order or discipline these facts by logic to create meaning; and they create their values through their imaginative powers, their visions. Each area of the curriculum, hopefully grouped into the largest manageable bundles, could plan for the involvement of the student in facts, logic, and imaginative power within their separate domains.

Science is as much a matter of imagination and purpose as it is of fact

---

[10] Earl Johnson, "The What of Core," paper delivered at the Core Curriculum Conference, Milwaukee, Wisconsin, October 16, 1965.

and logic. Literature has its special imaginative impact by the building of concrete details and ordered patterns. The commonality of these uses of human power could be planned for and related to each other in the texture of a curriculum plan.

Perhaps most important of all is what one might call the language of the disciplines. In an age of specialization and great knowledge growth many scholars have apparently forgotten the nature of all disciplines—as special languages to deal in special ways with aspects of reality. Awareness of the metaphorical nature of our discipline languages and the special perspectives each brings to common aspects of reality would be of great benefit for communicating the relatedness of the disciplines to each other.

RELATEDNESS IN INSTRUCTION

At the instructional level the problem of making a personal sense out of instructional activity is facilitated greatly by a coherently related curriculum plan. Yet, beyond this there is a crucial problem for the person in the curriculum.

Instruction is the interaction between persons, materials, ideas, performances, and objects of the contrived curriculum environment. This is not, however, a free-floating process. The school via its appointed and sometimes anointed agents (most frequently the teacher) attempts to influence the interaction. Instruction has a focus, and the focus is most often called children's *learning*.

The concept of children's learning, as it is utilized today, is the largest single instructional deterrent to the development of personal knowledge in students. It is, in fact, often due to this unfortunate focus that the travesty of much schooling is exposed. To assume that children's learning is a controllable outcome of curriculum and instruction is *impractical, unintelligent,* and *personally disastrous* for the student.

It is impractical because neither the school nor its agent have direct access to or control over the predispositions for learning that students bring to school. Thus, it is possible for Bloom[11] to provide a well-documented volume which indicates at its very least that the relationship between instructional activity and the development of intelligence and academic achievement is a tenuous one. For example, it is possible that children would not learn to read if they did not have instruction; but the quality of learning, the depth of skill, the commitment to ideas, and the personal

---

[11] Benjamin Bloom, *Stability and Change in Human Characteristics* (New York: John Wiley and Sons, 1964).

meaning of knowledge are essentially beyond the direct manipulative control of the teacher.

Our common sense observations of student performance are misleading. When we present a task to a student and the student goes through the required steps or activities and can give the expected responses on a test, we tend to assume that we have taught the responses. This suggests a lack of humility on our part and a rather startling display of ignorance concerning the relevant variables in learning. We may take credit for putting the student in contact with the task, but the learning that results is essentially beyond our control. The teacher has no direct access to the personal meaning systems of students, which can be readily witnessed by the wide divergence of values, past experiences, motivation, perceptions, and purposes found in students.

The concept of children's learning as the criterion measure of instruction is also personally disastrous to students. It places them in a position whereby their dignity, integrity, and personal worth are violated continuously. There are, at present, literally hundreds of studies which demonstrate the existence of prejudicial factors in school achievement. This list includes such factors as race, class, ability, and even sex at some levels and in some areas of the curriculum. One can only surmise what possible effect this myth of control may have upon a single person.

Our schools have been subverted by a concept of quality control where none exists. A set of technical, efficiency-oriented values—an economic metaphor, if you wish, lifted from an assembly line mentality—has been projected upon the living substance of persons in school settings.

What we do have control over, and what can be a positive force for persons in schools, are conditions for learning. Teachers can develop rules or norms to live by; they can create patterns of interpersonal relationships. Teachers can be selected with certain qualities, and wide varieties of choice are open in the selection and use of materials, methods, and media in instruction. Instruction which is based upon the creation of conditions for culturing rather than upon the outcomes of performance is both realistic and moral. It is instruction characterized by *beginnings* rather than *endings*.

Peters[12] has characterized education as the process of *initiation,* and it is this quality that is the foremost concern to the person. Peters says:

> I have remarked before that "education" implies standards, not necessarily aims. It consists in initiating others into activities, modes of conduct and thought which have standards written into them by reference

[12] R. S. Peters, "Education An Initiation," *Philosophical Analysis and Education* (New York: The Humanities Press, 1965).

to which it is possible to act, think, and feel with varying degrees of skill, relevance, and taste.[13]

and

> Education, then, can have no ends beyond itself. Its value derives from principles and standards implicit in it. To be educated is not to have arrived at a destination; it is to travel with a different view. What is required is not feverish preparation for something that lies ahead, but to work with a precision, passion, and taste at worthwhile things that lie to hand.[14]

Rules of thumb, or principles of instruction, are of little value for the task of initiation. If the person is to choose wisely, he must be initiated into the widest variety of alternatives possible. This in essence means the provision of the richest, most varied environment possible, and the utilization in instruction of a wide variety of techniques and media by which the environment may be known to the student as a source of alternatives. There is a distinct difference between "teaching" the environment and "teaching" the student how to see what is in the environment.

In concrete terms this would mean a great many more activities in schools that are entered into in the spirit of play—not in a frivolous sense, but as a free, spontaneous expression of human vitality and imagination. It is just this quality of playfulness that frees one from the massive weight of conditioned perceptions, and it is the lack of playfulness in our culture that prompts Europeans to remark that Americans "work" at play.

The suggestion of play is not intended necessarily to carry the connotation of creativity. There may well be times when play *is* creative. However, in mundane terms what is intended is simply the opportunity for students to come into contact with some substance of the world with a release from the pressures of sharply focused instructional objectives or specific evaluations of performance. Thus, instructional activity would be immeasurably improved for the person if it focused more directly upon initiating and introducing rather than upon concluding and evaluating.

Even with alternatives the student must be free to choose. This freedom in the instructional setting must arise from a release from the personal threat of other persons and imposed tasks, and through the development of inner resources or values by which the student can guide his own selections in his own best interests. Thus, release from social coercion in curriculum tasks and active value clarification are essential ingredients for instruction.

[13] *Ibid.*, p. 107.
[14] *Ibid.*, p. 110.

The teacher cannot coerce productivity. It is the discipline of the task, or the standards inherent in the immersion in the task, that are freely chosen from among alternatives and that have been clarified in terms of their personal relevance to the knowledge systems of the students which provide the form of personally acceptable coercion.

The role of the teacher in relation to the person in the curriculum is crucial. Much has been said and considerable research is being carried out in relation to teaching. One major finding is the rather large proportion of time teachers talk in classrooms. To illustrate the position taken here, it seems apparent that teachers' talk is not "good" or "bad" in and of itself. Talking and showing or demonstrating are not violators of persons by themselves. It is, instead, the instructional purposes of such teacher talk that are crucial or questionable. To tell students what is in the world and to show them how men know or create this knowledge is an essential part of the teaching role. To expect, however, that this process is a transmission of direct information from the teacher to the pupil's personal structure is senseless. Talk is one of the vital ways teachers have for describing the features of the "map" of culture and pointing out the principles of navigation.

Studies of teaching behavior today reveal a rather startling fact—the fact of similarity in interaction patterns regardless of the system of analysis utilized. The largest portion of teacher activity consistently revealed by these studies can be called lecturing and giving directions. A very small part of the reported behavior could be called stimulating, initiating, supporting, accepting, or clarifying.

James Raths[15] has distinguished two clarifying modes—the *reflective* and the *dissonant,* which would appear to facilitate the kind of person-oriented teaching behavior that is supported here.

In the reflective mode teachers tend to stimulate students to search for their own personal meanings and values. They may ask for expansion of student views, interpretations, definitions, summarizations of what they have said, and to listen to the views of others. The teacher is essentially supportive; his contributions are oriented toward serving to focus a student on the *meaning* of his thoughts. The teacher is also non-judgmental.

The dissonant mode suggested by the work of Festinger,[16] and according to Raths,[17] begins where the reflective mode ends. It is, in essence, the

[15] James Raths, "Clarifying as Reflecting and Dissonanting," paper delivered at the University of Wisconsin at Milwaukee, October 27, 1965.

[16] L. Festinger, *A Theory of Cognitive Dissonance* (Stanford, Calif.: Stanford University Press, 1957).

[17] Raths, *op.cit.,* p. 2.

stimulation for growth arising from the newly clarified values of the student. It is the impetus for encouraging the student to reformulate and incorporate new meanings into his self. The dissonant mode challenges the student to look again at his meanings of the world.

Teachers may enter a dissonant mode by asking for or pointing out alternatives to students' views, by noting inconsistencies in students' views, by challenging assumptions, sources of data or methods of student inquiry. The key to discontinuing this mode is the arousal of defensive reactions in persons. Both modes should be used in an open fashion, exempting no fact or concept from challenge, nor excluding any viewpoint from inquiry.

EVALUATING THE PERSON IN THE CURRICULUM

In curriculum as in most human endeavors, the place where values show are the critical points where judgments and evaluations are made. It is for this reason that the real meaning of a curriculum plan or instructional activity is often best understood in its evaluation phases.

An evaluation of the activity of the person in curriculum is necessary as long as one accepts the basic premise of the legitimacy of social influence in the schools. The character of this evaluation may vary radically, however. The phases of the *person* in activity are essentially different from the external rigor of stating objectives, selecting experiences, organizing experiences, and evaluating. Personal activity is characterized by a cycle of (1) initiation, (2) involvement, (3) self-direction, and (4) production. If teachers in instruction are truly concerned about the person, they will be continually assessing this flow of activity. During initiation phases they will focus upon the choice behavior of students. They will look for the free choosing from among alternatives and mediate their own actions in accord with this. When involvement or engagement is under way, the presence of productive tension is crucial. Teachers will look for bodily attitudes, verbal responses, and manipulative activity which suggests immersion in the task.

As the tasks progress the teacher must be alert for signs of self-direction. If students are unwilling or unable to keep themselves involved and focused, *then* the teacher must alter her actions in accordance with this assessment.

The final phase, production, means the concluding of some personally rewarding activity in the form of some coherently ordered product. It is not the quality of the product itself that is of crucial concern, but the culmination of the discipline of resolving some encounter with ideas, materials, or other persons that provides the key to evaluation.

When initiation falls upon deaf ears, or involvement is lacking, or self-direction and productivity are minimal, then teacher evaluation should serve as a basis for altering the tasks in school to bring about these phases of activity. The phenomenological fact, to the person of the student, is awareness of feelings of pleasure, satisfaction, joy, wonder, or awe, or the positive tension which he experiences.

COMMON MISUSE OF PERSON-ORIENTED POSITION

It is interesting to note that the person-oriented value position is often misused in curriculum thinking. Frequently, the concept (or some concepts) of individualized instruction and teacher-pupil planning are thought to be person-oriented. In many instances of either activity this is not the case.

There is, of course, no denying that what usually goes on in our schools is unbashedly directive, manipulative, and essentially sterile. What is perhaps more dangerous is the lip service given a person-oriented position when it is in fact not the case.

Much programmed instruction is of this character. To simply go *alone* to a task is not enough. To be self-paced rather than paced by the teacher's idea of some mythical norm may have its advantages, but it does not in any sense provide insurance against the violation of the integrity of the person. Further, to individualize programs in the sense that students may achieve similar goals by a variety of sensory routes does not catch the intention of a person-oriented position. As long as goals are prescribed and the student has no self-selection of purposes, there is an invasion of the person.

Much teacher-pupil planning is also characterized by this invasion. Either the teacher manipulates the group subtly or the aggressive persons in the group assert their leadership and coerce the others. In neither case can it be said that respect for the person is paramount.

Perhaps the most truly promising possibility in instruction is pluralism. Pluralism in this sense would mean the existence of multiple possibilities for student choice, within the same school and between schools. Nothing can be as potentially disastrous to the person as being trapped in a specific activity, a specific classroom, or even a specific school. A plurality of opportunities open to choice could be provided for students, whereby they could move freely in the context of a flexibly organized school environment.

Pluralism, as used here, would imply that there be no common set of curriculum expectations for each person. It would further imply that the development of fundamental tools for learning would be in the service of the person rather than the school system. The organizational structure would by necessity be framed loosely, and a variety of substantive areas and activities would be accessible and available at all times for as long as the student were committed to the pursuit of them.

At the risk of being misinterpreted, and by analogy, it is suggested that school should be more like a carnival and less like a concentration camp. Surely, the free movement and stimulation of varieties of enticing activities, in a carnival spirit, is more human than the degradation, manipulation, and confinement found in the quality of life in the concentration camp.

Our schools today are neither carnivals nor concentration camps, and it is well that this is so. For the carnival lacks serious purpose and the concentration camp has an only too well known and horrifying purpose. Yet the vitality and stimulation of the carnival atmosphere could be captured in the schools by the provisions of choice, freedom, and pluralistic opportunities for students.

THE BASIC FUNCTION OF THE SCHOOL

In conclusion, then, I would like to suggest that the logical outcome of a person-oriented curriculum position leads one to a redefinition of the function of the school in our society.

Our present society uses the schools for its economic purposes. The schools are seen as training grounds for the production of role players who will become doctors, lawyers, teachers, engineers, scientists, etc. Pressures growing from our *needs* for national security are part of this role concept of the person as a performer. The mass media project what Jules Henry[18] calls a philosophical system of advertising upon the members of society. The basic purpose of this pressure is to create in all persons a similar set of habits and desires. Urbanization has further forced a restriction on the person and the necessity for specialization in order to survive, and the coming automation in life can only accentuate the trend toward a segmented, dehumanized, impersonal concept and fact of living.

The schools are perhaps the only potentially controllable agency for humanization left in society. The schools, then, can play a major part in buttressing the person from the massive dehumanization of the broader society.

The basic function of the schools should become not the development of cultural intellect, or the production of specialists, or the creation of problem solvers or the developers of personality integration, but something in essence much simpler and a great deal more difficult. The schools should

[18] Jules Henry, *Culture Against Man,* (New York: Random House, 1963).

function to *protect the person* from dehumanization. They should "culture" the person until he has developed a reasonable sense of integrity and self worth, a coherent set of values and personal goals with which survival in our modern age as a human being is at least possible. We will create our own image of ourselves through the ways we structure and relate to our world. This image is presently in dire peril of becoming characterized by a partially ordered and conditioned set of regimented performances in the modern age. What we must strive for is to make men what they ought to be—complete human beings.

TECHNOLOGY
AND INSTRUCTION

Edward J. Green

The history of theorizing in the behavioral sciences and education is a kaleidoscope of shifting emphases and orientations of theoretical development. It is difficult to relate the results of many researches conducted within differing contexts. One would hope that one contribution of an emerging technology of instruction would be the organization of information into a coherent, systematic structure that enables one to relate one part to another. Before examining a possible approach to this objective, we may wish to explore briefly the place of technology in relation to the practice of instruction.

It is not appropriate to expect that a *theory* of educational technology will emerge as a result of our own or any other person's labors. Theory does not develop at the level of practice. Theory has to do with the substructure of conceptual organization in basic science. It has a contribution to make to technology by extension to specific conditions, but practice both in education and in clinical work involves a kind of engineering. We do not expect to see a theory of bridge building. What must emerge, however, is a systematic organization which brings together knowledge from a number of different fields of study.

Technology in education, then, is the systematic application of basic knowledge. It is manifest in the employment of various tools. Technology is sometimes regarded as synonymous with the tools employed. However, our position is that technology is not the teaching machine; it is not the

Edward J. Green is the Executive Officer of the Institute of Educational Technology and Professor of Education at Teachers College, Columbia University.

overhead projector, tape recorder, or closed circuit television; it is not the teacher. Rather it is the systematic use of any and all devices and media within a contrived sequence of instruction based upon sound engineering principles.

One might hope that the systematization of knowledge in the field of instruction might take the form of a handbook wherein, for a given instructional goal, it may be possible to prescribe appropriate sequences, media, and other relevant procedures to establish successfully a new behavioral repertory in the student.

Central to the development of an educational technology are the contributions of behavioral science. One of the first contributions has been the application of test theory in education. The ramifications of this development, as we all know, are extensive. They have helped to define the development of American education during the first quarter of the twentieth century. A second development, or application, of behavioral science is programmed instruction. It is only beginning to exert its influence.

Perhaps the most disconcerting aspect of the development of programmed instruction has been the lack of a rationale providing direction as to its significance, its usefulness, its possibilities, and the appropriateness of its application within the instructional community. The lack of a systematic organization of knowledge makes difficult the determination of any meaningful relation between programmed instruction and more conventional methods of teaching. In fact, there exists no coherent system of knowledge that relates any method of learning to any other. If we are to exploit the information that is available to us, we must elevate instruction to the status of a technology. If this is to come about there must be a systematic organization of the knowledge upon which it is based, so that rational decisions may be made regarding the appropriateness of various techniques and sequences of instruction.

The form the system ultimately will take obviously cannot be anticipated at the present time. One thing is clear: whatever form the system takes it will necessarily emerge as the consequence of rigorous logical, and perhaps mathematical, analysis. The formulations presented here are offered, not with the presumption that they represent the necessary form a coherent system of instruction will take, but rather as a prototype, the example of which may be followed in a full-scale effort at organizing existing knowledge. It is with full realization of the inadequacies of the primitive level of our own thinking at this time that we modestly propose consideration of this miniature system.

Let us make at the beginning what seems to be a plausible assumption that the instruction molecule is an event occurring between a learner and his instructional environment, whatever the properties of that environment may be. We will attempt to build upon this smallest unit of interaction a system which will have implications for educational practice that may be useful in organizing and systematizing our present state of knowledge and which should generate experiments that will in turn modify the model toward increased efficiency in its systematization and prediction. We will refer to this smallest unit as the *instructional opportunity*. It is the minimal behavioral segment wherein learning occurs.

We can also adopt as a descriptive approach a probability learning model as the formal description of the learning process.[1] We do this with the knowledge that other models are equally reasonable and equally plausible, and with the realization that perhaps the most efficient way of proceeding would be not to adopt any theoretical model whatsoever.

We are aware of the limitations of interpreting any gross instructional situation in terms of a probability learning model. We are aware that the model has real meaning only in terms of those highly specialized experimental contexts in which it may be tested. We are aware of the epistemological relationship between such a model and the physical world. But a start must be made somewhere, and we propose at least in the beginning that a loose correspondence between model and reality be considered so that predictions of an ordinal type may be generated.

A number of probability learning models have been developed describing the course of two-person interaction where various restraints upon the conditions of interaction are imposed.[2] We will consider briefly a model which purports to describe the course of interaction between two individuals where the behavior of one alters the probability of the other and vice versa. The action of each reinforces the action of the other.

An intransitive relationship is characteristic of all non-responsive learning environments and is also typical of the student-teacher relationship where the teacher's behavior is governed completely by external factors. For example, in mathematics no amount of persuasion on the part of the student should alter the teacher's position that 2 plus 2 equals 4 rather than 25. The probability of the instructor's reinforcing a particular student response is based upon information external to the interaction. The interaction from the point of view of the student must remain one of accommodation to a set of fixed values.

Our general concern must be with the situation where interaction be-

[1] W. K. Estes and C. J. Burke, "A Theory of Stimulus Variability in Learning," *Psychological Review*, 60, 1953, pp. 276–286.

[2] R. C. Atkinson, G. H. Bower, and E. J. Crothers, *An Introduction to Mathematical Learning Theory* (New York: John Wiley and Sons, 1965).

tween individuals results in changes in the behavior of both individuals. We assume that a learner encounters a learning task and discriminates, sees, perceives, or in the language of the model, samples, a certain fixed proportion of the total stimuli available on a given occasion. The response he makes in that setting, then, is conditioned to the elements which he has just sampled. The gradual course of learning is, in this statistical sampling model, accounted for by the fact that in order for the probability of a given response to reach 1.00 it is necessary that all the elements in the setting be sampled and the response be conditioned to them. With any fixed proportion of elements sampled in a particular setting, the probability of sampling new elements on succeeding trials approaches 0.00 asymptotically as the trials proceed, so that the nearer the learner approaches perfect performance, the more slowly does he approach it. Probability of response is defined as the ratio of conditioned elements to the total set of elements presented to the learner on a given occasion.

Let us regard the behavior of an individual as categorized into two mutually exclusive classes of R and $\bar{R}$. Let the behavior of a second individual be categorized into similar classes R' and $\bar{R}'$. Furthermore, let us assume that instances of behavior R, on the part of individual A, reinforce the behavior R' on the part of individual B. Similarly, instances of behavior R' on the part of individual B reinforce behavior R of individual A. Symmetrically, instances of $\bar{R}$ reinforce behavior $\bar{R}'$ and vice versa. The rate of learning is a function of the probability individual elements have of being sampled. It can be shown that where individual A and B each has equal resources for providing reinforcement for the behavior of the other, the terminal performance of the pair converges. The point of convergence is a function of the initial probabilities of the two individuals and of their respective rates of learning. Certain interesting predictions may be derived where arbitrary values are assigned to these constants.

Individuals may exert differing degrees of power within the group. Clearly, one of the most fundamental differences in the degree of power exerted is the possibility the individual has for reinforcing the behavior of the other person. This model naturally has cogency for the field of small group interaction specifically and for social psychology in general, but as learning in groups involves the same social processes as do other tasks performed by groups, the model has direct relevance to education. The relevance may be spelled out by reference to some of the implications for the social dynamics of group interaction. Let us consider the question of power. A slower learner in a real sense may be said to possess greater power or dominance in the group. In the case of the intransitive interaction, the validity of this is clear. Since in this situation the instructor has a contrived sampling ratio of 0.00, he controls the magnitude of change in the learner's behavior while his own response probabilities change not at all. This definition of power implies that a slower man will dominate a faster in the sense that the terminal position of the pair will be nearer the original position of the slower man than of the faster. Common sense objections can be raised to this interpretation of power, but it is emphasized that this condition exists where both individuals have equal resources for reinforcing behavior of the other. If one accumulates material resources as a consequence of reinforcement derived from one's own action, then a faster learner can produce an imbalance in the initial equalities by his more rapid accumulation. Therefore, unless this limitation is enforced through experimental control, the equality of resource condition is unstable and should be subjected to theoretical analysis in its own right.

It is possible to generalize to the N-person case. Individual A, who is designated the controllee, will interact with each member of an N-person group equally often. For present purposes it may be assumed further that the controllee interacts with only one member of a group at a time. Granting equal sampling ratios for all individuals in a situation, the group may be regarded as a single individual interacting with the controllee as before, with one important difference, over a series of n interactions with the controllee. Each member of the group interacts or is exposed to conditions leading to a change of the group members' behaviors only n/N times. In consequence, the mean rate of change is less for the group members than for the controllee. Furthermore, the larger the group, the less change will occur in the behavior of the controllers. With very large groups the individual exerts practically no effect upon the group, but inevitably conforms to the probability equilibrium previously established within the group. When learning rates are equal among members of the group and when reinforcing potentialities are equal, the stable terminal response probability for such a group is the mean of the various initial response probabilities of its members. From this it is seen that an accidental grouping of, say, two persons in initial response probability in a three-person group is most likely to bring a third, whose initial probability is far removed, nearer the two. That is, the terminal behavioral distribution of the group will be most heavily weighted by a homogeneous subset of its members. Here we may fruitfully relate researches on social conformity and homogeneous groupings of students.

In consideration of the N-person group, we may examine it from the opposite side where the controllee is a member of a group of N persons as it interacts with an instructor. In this case the instructor may interact in accordance with the intransitive situation. The instructor's position does not change, but the position of each member of the group is brought into conformity with the arbitrary standard he represents. We may ask what the effect is upon the learner when he is required to share the opportunities for interaction with $(N-1)$ other members of a group as opposed to the case where he and the instructor alone comprise the group.

The social implications of this for instruction are extensive. It is seen that there are differential predictions of the effectiveness of an instructional environment where the group is more or less heterogeneously composed, both in terms of initial response probability or, in the jargon of programmed instruction, in terms of their entering behaviors, and in terms of their learning abilities. Both of these factors are represented in the initial probabilities and the learning rate quantities. Again we would emphasize that we are not concerned with the adequacy of the present or of any particular model as a descriptive tool appropriate to any and all learning situations. We are using it rather as a device for formalizing relationships among instructional variables, for generating new experimental hypotheses and questions, and, perhaps most importantly, for sharpening the concepts which we use in analyzing an instructional setting.

As an example, we see that the frequency with which an individual in a large group is able to make use of instructional opportunities is a function of two parameters. One is the number of other students in the group; the other is the distribution of instructional opportunities over the members of the group. For example, additional students reduce the frequency, all things being equal, with which any one of them has opportunities to interact with the instructor, as contrasted with the case where the individual interacts upon every occasion as in a two-person group. Realistically, however, the distribution of these opportunities over a group is not flat but is highly skewed, so that a few individuals share the largest number of instructional opportunities while most persons in the group have access to a relatively smaller number of such opportunities. The function describing this distribution is readily obtainable from direct observation of student-teacher interaction in any classroom. Its form must be a function of such student variables as entering behaviors and equality of learning abilities, and will be altered in certain ways by these variables.

As the highest proportion of these instructional opportunities will be shared by those individuals who are most adequately prepared, either in terms of their initial level of sophistication or in terms of their ability to benefit from such interaction, and as those individuals who are least well equipped or prepared will have the least opportunity to benefit from such instructional opportunities, the initial imbalances in the equalities of students of varying backgrounds and ability ranges must inevitably be exaggerated. Common sense tells us that factors such as these contribute to the problems of the culturally disadvantaged child. Hopefully, analysis of the effect of differential interactions may suggest new approaches to the rectification of the unfavorable effects of such uncontrolled classroom practices. We propose to study these relationships with a view to determining procedures for insuring the optimal structure of such a group and perhaps to determine the procedures which will insure that the optimal structure will be used in actual practice.

With the increase of other individuals in the learning environment, there is necessarily an increased number of effective stimuli impinging upon an individual learner. If, as in the probability learning model, we take as the theoretical definition of the sampling ratio the ratio s/S, where s is the number of stimuli samples, and S is the total number of effective stimuli present in the environment, increasing the total number of effective stimuli reduces the rate of learning. In other words, inclusion of a large number of distracting stimuli decreases the rate of learning. In terms of these two facts, namely, the decrease in the number of learning opportunities brought about by the individual's being placed in a large group of students and the decrease in his rate of learning caused by the increase in extraneous stimuli, we have a rational explanation for the fact that individualized instruction is efficient. This is true simply because the opportunity for interaction with the instructor and for appropriate reinforcement through confirmation or disconfirmation is fractionated by the number of students in a class. The fact of limited opportunity for interaction produces a slowdown in the rate of learning for the class as a whole and for any individual student in it, as contrasted with the case where a teacher allows the student every opportunity to make a response to him and to the material.

When a student is placed in the programmed instructional setting, either with or without the assistance of a machine, the range of stimuli is considerably reduced. The result is an effective increase in the sampling ratio. The changes produced in the sampling ratio by these different learning situations is directly related to the questions of channel capacity in communication theory terms. A wide range of experiments is suggested, wherein the rate of change of the material presented is empirically altered to determine the channel capacity of individuals differing in initial accomplishment or entering behaviors and in their ability to make use of new information.

The parameters of the instructional machinery may also be subjected to experimental analysis within this context. For example, we are aware that the opportunity for interaction is an essential variable in the learning setting. To what extent, therefore, must we balance instructional opportunities of this type against the advantage of increasing the channel capacity through the use of new media of instruction such as television? There is undoubtedly an optimal point for a learner beyond which additional information is lost. It should be possible to determine not only the optimal rate of information presentation in terms of the channel capacity of the learner, but also the optimal trade-off between provision for interaction and the channel capacity.

Other variables may be studied equally well within the same rational framework as before. For example, the area of motivation is one which has been avoided assiduously, not only by proponents of programmed instruction, but also by behavioral scientists in general. This avoidance is largely the result of the absence of formal concepts in this area and the lack of agreement among behavioral psychologists as to the operational meaning of motivation.

Several authors have noted that the effectiveness of an instructional sequence depends upon the optimal balance between material being too simple on the one hand and too difficult on the other. In the development of programmed instruction, Skinner emphasized the importance of error-free performance. This led to emphasis upon small steps in the construction of program sequences. However, it was soon apparent that if the steps were too small, the program too trivial, then accomplishment in the program did not lead to effective learning. Apart from the fact that a low error rate may be achieved at the expense of instruction altogether, a teacher program that moves too slowly for a higher calibre student may be ineffective as a teaching instrument. In the probability model, we may find some elucidation of the factors governing this state of affairs. It has been proposed that reinforcement be interpreted as a result of the organism reducing a gap between a prior- and a post-action state of affairs.[3] Learning is a sensitive form of this situation and requires that the learner recognize and discriminate his own state of knowledge and be capable of recognizing a change in it. Slow moving programs of any type are an insult to the intelligence of a bright student, and if not an insult, they may at best be relatively unstimulating. If a frame so constrains the range of possible responses that the correct one is inevitable, then probably the student hasn't learned much from making such a response. After all, there isn't a great deal of reinforcement, generalized or otherwise, to be derived from having accomplished something trivial. If generalized reinforcement is derived from accomplishing something, then the something must be worthwhile.

If we consider the behavior of a learner at an early stage of learning where his performance is far removed from the terminal criterion perfor-

[3] E. J. Green, *The Learning Process and Programmed Instruction* (New York: Holt, Rinehart, and Winston, 1962).

mance sought by the instructor, then we must see that the probability of his making the correct response in terms of criterion performance is very low. At the same time if we examine the typical learning curve, we see that the largest changes occur during the early interactions. If we attribute reinforcement to the recognition of the change, then the accomplishment of the learner during the early stages may be presumed to be relatively greater than it is during later stages. Let us postulate two factors relative to reinforcement. One is the probability of reinforcement, $p(S^R)$; the second we may call the measure of reinforcement, $m(S^R)$. It is with this second factor that we are concerned when we speak of motivation.

Complex relationships exist between these two aspects of reinforcement, but let us assume a simple relationship. If the probability of reinforcement is 1.00 given a correct response, then the probability of reinforcement equals the probability of response at a given stage. Let us set the value of reinforcement to be the amount of change produced at any stage of the learning process. We see, therefore, that the *probability* of reinforcement on the one hand increases as learning progresses, whereas the *measure* of reinforcement decreases as learning progresses. As the effectiveness of an individual reinforcement becomes less, the probability of the individual's receiving a reinforcement becomes greater. In the early stages of learning where the probability of reinforcement is low, the value of it on the other hand is very great.

We may speculate concerning the optimal conditions of reinforcement: What is the optimal trade-off of probability of reinforcement against the measure of reinforcement? In other words, how may we optimize learning by manipulating these quantities?

Preliminary investigation would lead us to believe that the optimal point is independent either of initial starting values or of the sampling ratios. It is a simple function of the probability of response as against the relative change, and seems to be at a point midway between the initial response value and the terminal response value. This suggests a rationale for setting optimal step-size in self-instructional programs and also suggests another mechanism that may contribute to the effectiveness of such self-instructional programs. Where the criterion is started low and progressively raised and where the ceiling is nevertheless kept high enough so as not to make attaining it trivial, we, in effect, are maximizing both probability and measure of reinforcement at each step, so that we anticipate the course of the learning curve and track the curve to its asymptote ahead of the normal course that would be followed if conventional instructional procedures were followed.

We must ask experimental questions of the indirect effects of various sequences upon the behavior of learners, particularly with regard to the question of creativity. Although there has been considerable concern with the importance of divergent thinking and creative approaches to problem-solving during recent years, true creativity is based upon a mastery of underlying fact. Michelangelo could not have created the works of art for which he is famous had he possessed the spontaneity and intellectual freedom of a chimpanzee. Genius lies in creating within the restraints imposed by various realities, formal or physical. The natural environment of the learner is so loaded with extraneous stimuli that it is unlikely that we shall ever achieve, even were it our intent, the homogeneous, concretized behavior which is so often regarded as the horrendous consequence of engineered instruction. The problem seems to be quite the contrary, namely, to employ what primitive techniques we have at hand to insure within reasonable bounds a minimum level of accomplishment. The questions relating to creativity certainly need experimental amplification, but unfortunately they also need a less murky formulation than they have enjoyed to date.

In addition to investigation of the behavioral and instructional components, an investigation of the relationships between these factors and economic considerations as they affect innovation and use in the educational structure as a whole must be undertaken. We must establish the value of instruction at all levels, in terms both of its value to the individual and its value to society. We must be concerned with the ways by which value balanced against cost restrains the development of the system. We will explore new approaches to education to determine what alternatives to the traditional school may be developed to maximize instructional effectiveness at minimal costs.

Economic considerations determine existing practices to an overriding degree. It may be anticipated that we may learn that optimal class size as we now recognize it represents a compromise among various cost factors. If it is possible to vary these factors, we may be able to find more efficient ways to utilize our resources. We have reason to believe from preliminary explorations that individualized instruction plays its most important role at a particular stage of instruction, and that other parts of the sequence are less sensitive to the advantages of individualized instruction. If this is true, it will be possible to develop strategies for using various media and types of control, both individualized and group-paced, that will lead to more efficient instruction.

This, then, is the broad design of technological development as we see it emerging over the next few years. Insofar as programmed instruction is concerned, its impact has yet to be assessed. It is entirely possible that within the next decade or two the programmed textbook as we know it today will have disappeared. If this is so, it will be no great loss if the essence of programmed instruction, namely, the application of behavioral engineering to instruction, has gained a foothold by way of this tool. There is no reason that the techniques of behavioral analysis and the empirical construction of instructional sequences cannot be extended to all phases of instruction. Probably the greatest contribution of programmed instruction will be exactly this kind of analysis and modification of instructional techniques. The program presented in the teaching machine or in the format of the programmed textbook only happened to be the physical form that this mode of attack took in its first approach to the problem. One would hope that more effective and certainly more stimulating products of this technology will develop over the coming years.

Technological growth has been so rapid and so poorly digested by civilization in general that we may anticipate a limitation upon our own growth if new means are not found to exploit this technology. We will find ourselves rapidly approaching a technological, ecological balance which must become a fatal stasis if new avenues of exploitation are not opened. These avenues can only be found and exploited through the fullest use of technology itself. If this organization of knowledge does not come about, if direction for future research is not provided, then we may very well choke on our own technological products.

Survival in the thermonuclear age depends upon our developing knowledge in behavioral science, which at least matches the state of knowledge in the physical sciences. So, in addition to the critical stage already being approached in the physical sciences with respect to indigestibility of information, we have imposed upon us the additional problem of bringing our social institutions to a level of competence adequate to deal with problems we face at the present time. If our present educational system deteriorates through the impact of larger numbers of students in the face of ever-diminishing opportunities for education, the battle is hopelessly lost, and the fate of western civilization is sealed.

CURRICULAR INSIGHTS
FROM EDUCATION OF
AMERICAN CHILDREN ABROAD

JOHN J. BROOKS

THE UNITED STATES has two centuries of experience in the absorption, accommodation, and integration of varied cultural elements that compose its population. This has not been a major concern of professional education until quite recently. We have invented a new set of slogans to serve as rubrics for the objects of our professional activity: "The Culturally Deprived Child," "The Disadvantaged Child," "The Child in the Slum Area," and so forth. Actually, what we are talking about with these euphemisms are the Negro, the Puerto Rican, and poor people!

By lumping all these problems together, some of us are bound to emerge with the idea that people who are economically impoverished are also culturally deprived. Poverty and cultural deprivation are not synonymous, however. If we become confused about this, we shall wind up providing these children with economic skills as we deprive them of their cultures.

A teacher in a Harlem school is depressed by the ineffective force represented by the father of one of her students. Transferred to a school in a privileged community in Westchester, she may remain blind to the fact that a father in *this* group catches the 7:10 in the morning, comes back from work late in the evening, goes out three nights a week, spends his weekends playing golf, and packs his son off to camp in the summer. Both of these fathers are ineffective, yet one of them is condemned on the basis of his poverty, or because he is Puerto Rican or Negro.

It is important to remember that a Puerto Rican child who comes to the United States (frequently to New York City) has a rich culture behind

JOHN J. BROOKS is Professor of Secondary Education at New York University.

him, which cannot be equated with the life of poverty that lies before him. It is very unfortunate that children who are "culturally different" in our public schools are also usually economically poor. Their well-to-do cousins, in lesser numbers, attend our private schools, where the confusion of economics and culture rarely occurs.

MAN AND CULTURE

Perhaps we need to review what we know about the nature of man and culture before we make a taurine tour of the porcelain in this situation.

Physicists today are devoted to inventing new devices to insure the extinction of our species. Perhaps this has spurred anthropologists to increase their efforts to clarify our origin.

A great deal of rich information is now being developed which remains unevaluated by our profession. Apparently most of the criteria by which we certified primitive man as separate from his primate cousins is no longer valid. Apartheid seems to be as difficult to handle in the Pleistocene as it is today in the manic scene. The old rule of thumb—of opposable thumbs —does not put the finger on our species. Apes possess four of these members and should be twice as adept in thumbing an evolutionary ride.

We are a tool-making species, though our products seem to relate more to the incineration than the ascension of man. In this genocidal century it is a little embarrassing to anoint ourselves as the animal that has reasoning powers. We are not the only animal that walks on his hind legs. Ostriches perform this feat also and may have one other behavior pattern in common with man. We are an animal that has speech. Other animals have developed this ability also. Perhaps our ancestors became especially skilled in communication because they anticipated the embarrassment of their descendants today and therefore invented speech to confuse their issue!

ANTHRO-APOLOGISTS

Our family escutcheon is pretty well blotted. In fact, it is a veritable Rorschach, providing fearful glimpses of a killer ape, brave enough to face a tiger, though the greater threat might be his brother behind his unprotected back. Perhaps the proper heraldic banner for our family tree should show a mutant anthropoid, rampant upon a field of atomic rubble.

So, the physicists continue to devise, and the anthropologists continue to dig, and there is a certain sporting aspect to the whole situation. We can only hope that there will be a scribe or two around who can make testament to our genesis before recording our exodus.

Perhaps what we need here is a new type of anthropologist—a benignant researcher, more gentleman than scholar, who can rearrange the evidence in our favor. We might call him an anthro-apologist.

THE ANIMAL WHO INVENTED HIMSELF

We have missed the basic characteristic that enables man to elect himself as the animal of distinction. Man has literally invented himself. His tiny inventions, in cumulative form, are called culture. Rob him of his culture and he is nothing.

The digger wasp, the stickle-back fish, and the sparrow are born educated. Most of what they are yet to be, they already are. Man is born without much more instinctive behavior than an underachieving earthworm. All that he is yet to be—he has yet to invent. The conception of man takes place in his mother's womb. The *concept* of man is a homemade product; it is based on the perceptions that a tribe has about its cumulative experience.

CREDO, ERGO SUM

When we deprive a group of its beliefs, we have robbed it of its being. Man is therefore not a species of opposable thumbs, but of opposable beliefs. He is not an animal which readily goes to war against a cousin of another color, but history is saturated with the blood of brothers who died in defense of their differing beliefs.

Considerations of this sort are difficult in the loaded setting of our own classrooms where we are attempting to get children to jettison the inventions of their community or their culture and replace this cargo with inventions that conform to our own standards.

Schools still cling, to some degree, to the idea that a good American is white, Protestant, has pioneer ancestors, possesses Puritan virtues, and will not do well until he is well-to-do.

To this school culture, we have added a classroom invention: this is the notion that if you measure the behavior of enough ten-year-olds you can determine the general characteristics of ten-year-olds. From this dubious conclusion, it is but a small leap to the concept that therefore any child who does not conform to these general statistics should be sent to the guidance office.

CHANGING LITTLE DEARS INTO LITTLE GESELLS

Puerto Ricans, an affectionate people, go on raising their children as little dears. In the United States, however, we are beginning to raise our little dears as little gesells. It is difficult to get a good fix on what we are doing while we are engaged in attempting to make awkward Americans out of adept Puerto Ricans. It is virtually impossible to make an impartial appraisal of an intercultural situation when the unannounced objective is to lift "lower cultures" up to the fine, high place of American culture.

THE OVERSEAS SCHOOL

There is, however, a fine laboratory for experimentation with intercultural situations. This laboratory is represented by the recent development of some two hundred American-sponsored elementary and high schools, situated in some sixty countries of the world.

Unlike our military dependent schools abroad, these civilian, parent-sponsored schools enroll children of many, many cultures. Any teacher in these schools, whether American or not, is facing an intercultural situation which does not contain the confusing elements of different economic status, of immigration, of neighborhood dynamics, and so forth. The major thing that is different among these children is simply their differing cultural backgrounds.

A CONFUSION OF INVENTIONS

An American teacher, in this setting, teaching a mixed fourth- and fifth-grade group, begins to have a sense of cultural deprivation herself. As she looks at these "tens" and "elevens," she vigorously reviews her child studies. "At this age," she quotes to herself, "children are untidy, overabundant in energy, and accident-prone." Her eyes light on an Asian child, hands folded in comfortable immobility, with all his itchy muscles apparently stored in his locker.

"Children are highly critical of their families at this age," she states to herself firmly. She is looking at a Bedouin child who has just finished a moving recital of his pride in and affection for his family *and* his tribe.

"Relationship to group and the desire for approval by peers is vitally important at this age," she remembers, as she observes the son of an African chief. She remembers the African chief very well. He has told her, "You mustn't mind if my boy has little to do with his classmates. Among our people, boys his age want to spend all their time with adults and are strongly intent on becoming identified with the adults as quickly as possible."

PARENTS ENGAGE IN UN-AMERICAN ACTIVITIES

Parents in the overseas school are a little amused by the idea of parent conferences. In fact, they are somewhat startled by the way Americans tend to make the school a central consideration of the community. However, they suffer the annoyance and even find that it helps them to express their confusion to the American teacher: "I really don't understand why my child has such poor marks on his report card," says one Oriental parent. "I have taught him to remain silent, never ask questions, memorize faithfully, and remain passive under all circumstances. I am sure that he follows my instructions, yet you have given him bad grades in everything except his tests. I happen to know that a young American friend of his, who is also in your class, received excellent grades, yet he is aggressive, talkative, constantly asking questions, and is always getting first in line. I am sure that you have no racial prejudice, but how else can I explain this contradiction?"

The harassed teacher in this situation will hardly think of these children as "culturally deprived," because they come to school in limousines. She may begin to accept the fact that they are culturally different. She may eventually stop trying to make second-rate Americans out of first-class Orientals.

She, herself, is constantly forced to make adjustments to the host-culture in which she is a guest for the year. She begins to develop a great deal of empathy for human beings who are forced to adjust to their host-culture in America.

If she is really wise, she will not spend her energies attempting to work out coexistent intercultural situations. She will do what human beings have always done: set about the business of inventing a new culture that has new components.

She will develop some dubiety about child-studies, because she will begin to understand that such studies may begin with the behavior of children, but will most certainly end by becoming a cultural force that invents a special species of child.

If her school provides an IQ test, based on colors, patterns, and space relationships in order to leap the language barrier, she will soon discover that these tests are measurements of cultural inventions. Japanese children will prove brilliant because their culture includes images of man delighting in color, patterns, and arrangements. Arab children will fail these tests, because their backgrounds involve a dun-colored world without graven images.

A CURRICULUM SHOULD INCLUDE . . .

Beyond these lessons, she may have a growing understanding of ways to meet problems at home. She may begin by giving an A to the Chinese boy because he is attentive, thoughtful, and absorptive. She will also give his American classmate an A because he is interrogative, argumentative, and creative. The values of both are to be cherished.

"Wouldn't it be wonderful," she muses, "if the curriculum at home could make provision for the encouragement of such a range of characteristics?" Such a curriculum would revive a few basic questions that have echoed down the centuries: "Who is the good citizen?" "Who is the happy man?" "What is the good [sic] Society?"

These questions cannot be answered by quoting such granitic Vermont virtues as "effective citizenship" or "worthy home membership." Even that most forbidding of Puritan pronouncements, "The worthy use of leisure time," may have to go, despite its echo of salvation and rich redundancy. We may have to allow some members of the congregation to follow after false idleness or engage in periods of non-immoral inactivity.

As this century of cultural confrontation proceeds, across the continents and in our classrooms, we shall have to add more and more multiple choices in our tests of man. For the moment, it is true, we may have to engage in a great deal of busy work that represents a by-product of the predicaments in our classroom. But eventually we must remember that our job is not to teach whites and blacks to make accommodations to each other, nor is it to visit the virtues of the fathers upon their sons unto the third generation, nor to disenfranchise the stranger within our gates.

Eventually we must remember what kind of an animal we are. We are the animal that invents itself, and we are capable of marvelous inventions. If we are still the forest ape, then we can allow the emerging culture to reflect our jungle fears and forest fevers. But you and I do not struggle in the thicket. We dwell in the groves of academe, where we can invent wonderful fruit from our labors. Here in these groves we must set about inventing a promising tomorrow, with a sun that reflects the best of each of us. Here in the groves of academe, we remember with Frost, our woods are lovely, dark, and deep.

But we have promises to keep and dreams to make before we sleep.

PROSPECTS FOR
CURRICULUM CHANGE
IN TEACHER EDUCATION

MARGARET LINDSEY

IN A SERIOUS discussion among a group of professional educators the other day one member confessed, "I'm worried; I'm baffled; I'm frightened; I feel uninformed." He was referring to the impact of the federal government on the schools, particularly with respect to the increase and extension of categorical aid. Others sitting around the table were inclined to share his feelings, and there followed a long series of testimonials to the magnitude and the subtlety of the influence of the federal government's programming of financial aid to education. No one in the group would wish for less government responsibility in financing the nation's schools. They would all wish for more deliberate assessment of the scope and nature of the bits and pieces of influence. Without such assessment, one is worried, baffled, and frightened for fear he may wake up one morning to find the whole has been lost in the fragmented parts, that purpose has been drowned in a sea of isolated projects, and that people have been relegated to a low rung on the priorities ladder.

A team of three professors was recently engaged in planning for a class session in a course called Curriculum and Instruction in Higher Education. Their intent was to plan a way for initiating consideration of at least some of the factors that influence decisions in higher education. It was immediately apparent that it would be possible to deal with only a few representative forces in each of three large categories: external noneducational forces, external educational forces, and internal institutional forces. In the

MARGARET LINDSEY is Professor of Education at Teachers College, Columbia University.

first category are such factors as manpower needs, international involvement, automation, and urbanization. In the category of external educational forces, such factors as the United States Office of Education, graduate faculties, academic societies, and accrediting agencies appear. Influences within institutions come from administrators, students, faculty, and the priorities and values of each group, as well as of individuals within the groups.

The politics of education today is in such a state of ambiguity that legislators devote time to establishing lines of responsibility and authority for school boards and superintendents; governors sit in a council making decisions in areas formerly delegated to professionals with expertise; specialists in a wide range of fields turn their complete attention to the intriguing question of how decisions are made and innovations brought about in the educational program; and a foundation grants money to set up an institute to study the politics of education.

Every Tom, Dick, and Harry appears to have ideas about what the schools ought to do, in general and often in particular. If Tom happens to have the combination of circumstances that lend him power, his idea is heard; it is likely to be accepted by a few or by many, and it gets into practice somewhere. When Tom is thoughtful, when his motivations are ethical, when he works in concert with appropriate people who take into account pertinent knowledge and conditions, when he and they sustain their concern to the point of appraising honestly what is happening, and when he keeps his mind open to acceptance, modification, or rejection of his idea, the chances are that education gains. Tom, Dick, and Harry may be individuals or they may represent groups of scholars in education, scholars in a given discipline, specialists of any sort, or any other group of persons drawn together by common interest, concern, or activity.

One must have considerable courage to communicate to others what he sees as he gazes into his crystal ball in this kind of setting. The dynamism of factors operative today is such as to make uncertain any clear trends and to make foolish absolute confidence in predictions, except possibly the prediction that influential factors will multiply, their interrelationships and impact will increase, and the rate of change will accelerate. But we dare not cease to be concerned about the future because it is filled with uncertainty. We dare not do less than our best in taking advantage of our understanding of what is and in creating conditions that promise to make the future an improvement over the present. It is in this context that I want to make some predictions about teacher education in the immediate future. Before advancing these predictions, however, it is necessary to state three general assumptions.

PRELIMINARY ASSUMPTIONS

Public awareness of the importance of education to the nation and to the world has sharpened during the last decade. There are indications that the quality of education will be on the public conscience even more in the foreseeable future. The combination of public awareness and its expression in provision for better financing has served to heighten public interest in what goes on in schools. Citizens of tomorrow will be even more sensitive to their educational system, they will be more informed and more action-oriented in expression of their interest. They will place education high on the list of priorities at the local, state, national, and international levels. This is my first assumption.

The second assumption is that we will continue to have formally organized institutions called schools and colleges. Within these organized institutions we may see a "carnival" atmosphere (as Macdonald suggested), where multitudes of learning opportunities are available from which persons will select, as appropriate to their status in becoming complete human beings. We may see a technology of education so designed as to prescribe for every instructional goal appropriate kinds of sequences, appropriate media, and other relevant procedures (as Green suggested). We may find our present conceptions of school buildings, classrooms, and laboratories supplanted by new ideas on the physical setting for formal education. We may see presently unthought-of notions about the organization of pupils, about the timing of and time in school, about administrative structure, and about instructional material and procedures. But we will see schools, institutions formally organized to provide educational opportunity.

The third general assumption is that we shall continue to have in our schools a large corps of specialists called teachers, and that they will continue to be the single most important factor influencing the nature and quality of formal education. Innovations in school organization, in instructional media, in assignment of differentiated functions to teachers will be only as effective as teachers make them. An ungraded class will have no advantage, except as knowledgeable and skilled teachers capitalize on its unique features. A physical plant that has learning centers, individual carrels, television facilities, and other presently undreamed-of innovations will contribute to a better quality of education for youngsters exactly as much as teachers are able to take proper advantage of it—no more and no less. Curriculum proposals, by whomever they are advanced, will be implemented and tested in the schools only as teachers are willing and able to do so. In the final analysis, researching for better understanding of teaching, of learning, or of nurturing the becoming human being will find its significance as teachers are able to behave in ways appropriate to new findings. It is a generally accepted fact today that teachers hold the central position in the scheme of things designed to improve educational opportunity in the schools. Concerns about education quickly come to focus on the teacher, and quite naturally gravitate to questions about his selection, preparation, and performance. This focus will persist in the future.

SOME PREDICTIONS ABOUT THE EMERGING SETTING FOR TEACHER EDUCATION

A new atmosphere, full of promise, is in the making. A significantly modified setting for teacher education is emerging. I want to speculate about selected elements in this setting, to make some predictions.

CANDIDATES FOR TEACHING WILL BE INTELLECTUALLY ABLE AND HIGHLY MOTIVATED STUDENTS

To assume that education has high priority in the public conscience and that the quality of teachers and teaching is the single most important factor in the educational system is important. When things are viewed as important, they tend to receive attention. Important things are ascribed status and respect. It can be predicted, whatever the specific developments of the future, that teaching will be seen as one of the prestigeful professions. Members of it will be even more respected and rewarded than they are now.

Large groups of able young people will aspire to be admitted to the practice of education. Some will seek entrance into the profession on a "forced choice" basis, not because of lack of ability to be admitted to other professions (which is often now the case), but because alternative channels for their life work appear to diminish in number with the rise in automation and technology. Most, however, will seek entrance into teaching on the basis of first choice. These will be the young people who, seeking personal identity and worthy outlets for their deep commitments to make a difference in their world, will see teaching as a way of fulfilling themselves and their hopes.

For the most part, policies of selective admission to preparation for teaching and to practice have thus far remained at the talk level, their enforcement hampered by competition for services of able youth, by a real or imagined hierarchy among the professions, and by imbalance in supply and demand. The time is at hand now to make operative high standards in the selection and retention of candidates in teacher education. Admittedly we do not know all we need to know about predicting success in teaching, and we therefore cannot have complete confidence in rigid enforcement of single standards. To accumulate more knowledge on which to base standards is a task that has persisted a long time and will continue to confront us. But some knowledge is available, both from systematic studies and from the wisdom abstracted from experience. While pushing ahead in the search for new knowledge, action can be taken on what is already known. Given opportunity really to select candidates for teaching, and assuming that those responsible for selection have courage, we can project teacher education programs planned for students who have intellectual ability and whose motivations arise from conviction that teaching is important.

STUDY OF PEDAGOGY WILL RISE TO AN UNPRECEDENTED POSITION OF IMPORTANCE

Arguments that have long been advanced on the relative importance of knowledge of subject matter to be taught and knowledge about teaching have already ceased to have rational bases. Widespread recognition is now apparent that both are needed in substantial amounts, and the program of teacher education that does not assign appropriate status to both is less than adequate.

The present revival of interest in study of teaching has potential beyond earlier investigations which focused primarily on effectiveness. The main thrust of current studies is toward understanding the process of teaching and developing ways of examining that process in operation. These studies will provide new knowledge and a technology that can be used with students in preparatory programs. They will provide descriptive instrumentalities for investigation of relationships among teacher and pupil behaviors, and thus enable more systematic study by teachers of the effects of their behavior on what goes on in the classroom.

Skinner, in a recent article in *Saturday Review,* entitled "Why Teachers Fail," suggested that the cause of failure is largely inadequate attention to pedagogy. He laments the weakness of past programs in failing to provide any real study of teaching and notes that the task of programming instruction has once again called attention to the cruciality of teaching strategies.

Scholars in various fields of subject matter recommend that schools help pupils to develop key concepts and to gain understanding of the methods by which knowledge is discovered and verified in the several disciplines. Surely it must be recognized that this is as much a demand for emphasis on the ordering of content for teaching and on teaching methodologies as it is a demand that teachers have control over the subject matter they are to teach.

As a logical extension of curriculum-proposal making by scholars in academic disciplines and of their involvement in elementary and secondary schools, there will be a corps of academic scholars whose specialty will be "the teaching of" the subject. These will be persons who meet the requirements of scholarship in their respective fields of subject matter, but whose focus in preparation and in practice will be on the improvement of the teaching of the subject in the schools. Study of methods of teaching, now often in ill repute, will be a significant and demanding part of the preparation of all teachers.

Not to be overlooked in assessing the future status of study of pedagogy are some important additional factors, such as the outspoken criticism by college students of the low quality of teaching to which they are often subjected, and the tacit agreement among college and university officials that, although their faculty members know and are committed to their subject and their research, too many of them are deficient in teaching ability and commitment, and the interest and activity of professional schools of medicine, law, dentistry, and engineering in the selection and specialized preparation of teachers for these schools.

A cycle of relationships is already developing. Teaching gains prestige, more able persons become students of teaching, these more able persons are scholars who advance knowledge in important ways, and they and the focus of their scholarship gain in status. A new cycle follows immediately upon the old, and each raises the importance of systematic study of teaching to a higher level.

A NEW PARTNERSHIP WILL EXIST BETWEEN SCHOLARS IN ACADEMIC FIELDS AND SCHOLARS IN EDUCATION

Events of our time are a prelude to a new and different relationship between scholars in academic fields and scholars in education. One of the primary assets accruing from work of academic scholars on curriculum proposals is the changed concern of these persons about education in elementary and secondary schools. Even those college professors who once held a disdainful and negative attitude toward teachers and teaching in lower levels have made insightful discoveries as they tried to move into curriculum development and teaching in the schools. For many, this has been an abrupt awakening and a forceful challenge to their responsibilities. These persons will not soon again view themselves as completely removed from the problems of elementary and secondary schools and the programs designed to prepare teachers for those schools.

Two decades ago Lawrence Haskew proposed state councils on teacher education with membership from all segments of the profession. Soon thereafter the National Commission on Teacher Education and Professional Standards was born and precipitated similar organizations in the various states. Recently these commissions have, with belated wisdom, included in their ranks representatives from the academic disciplines. For some time now, it has been common practice in good institutions to view the preparation of teachers as an all-college function and to implement this view by establishing committees with representation from all parts of the college or university. In discharging their responsibility for making major decisions in teacher education programs, these committees have demonstrated the value of wide participation in planning and conducting programs.

Activities of such societies as the American Association for the Advancement of Science, the Foreign Language Association, and the Council of Learned Societies working jointly with professional groups in study of the preparation of teachers represent still another evidence of a new and different involvement of academic scholars in teacher education. In these activities, as in those related to curriculum proposals, some of these scholars have for the first time examined their specialties within the framework of total teacher education programs; some professional educators have, for the first time, come to understand the concerns of such scholars.

A NEW BREED OF PROFESSIONAL
EDUCATOR WILL BE ACTIVELY INVOLVED

The signs are already present that a new breed of professional educator is in the making. These will be educators whose scholarship is in the use of knowledge and methods of particular disciplines in the study of theory and practice in education. They will differ in important ways from those we have known in the past. Like the students who enter preparation for teaching, they will choose to prepare and to continue their careers as students of education, and they will have strong commitment and pride in their responsibility.

These educators will not be cast in the mold of professional educators who try now to deal with application of findings in foundational disciplines without adequate knowledge of the disciplines. Nor will they be cast in the die of present scholars in the disciplines who attempt to make proposals about the meaning of their findings for practice in the schools with too little knowledge of what goes on in schools. These will be persons who recognize a specialty within a specialty—scholars in sociology who specialize in education, scholars in political science who specialize in education, scholars in psychology who specialize in education. Graduate faculties will offer programs uniquely designed to prepare these scholars for careers in education. Their respective academic societies will recognize and respect their specialties in education, certainly beyond what is the case at present.

In all too many instances now in teacher education programs teaching assignments are made to persons inadequately prepared, either because they do not know enough about schools and teaching or because they do not have control over the basic discipline with which they are dealing. In the future, just as secondary school teachers will not be permitted to teach in fields where they are not specialized, so college teachers will not be permitted to teach educational psychology without specialization directly related to the assignment, nor to teach social foundations of education without complete competence to do so.

THE GENERALIST WILL HAVE
IMPORTANT AND UNIQUE RESPONSIBILITIES

It may appear paradoxical to suggest that the importance of the generalist in education will become greater in an age of increased specialization. It is nevertheless reasonable. Caswell noted that there are at least three concerns that are responsibilities of the curriculum worker: (1) to establish a consistent relationship between general goals, on the one hand, and specific objectives that guide teaching, on the other; (2) to assure sound sequence and continuity in the curriculum; and (3) to assure balance in the curriculum. Wann noted the great interest in curriculum reform of many groups both outside of and within the field of education and suggested that the curriculum as developed in American schools can become an even more hopeless hodgepodge of diverse goals and procedures than it now is; that packaged curriculum approaches leave little room for flexibility in adapting content and methods to the special needs of individuals or groups of learners; that proposed innovations in curriculum have frozen present school organization and have given tacit support to the status quo. In discussing a model for producing knowledge and theory with respect to educational technology, Green repeatedly recognized the multiple variables in pupils, conditions, materials, and so on. Macdonald's challenge to develop a person-oriented curriculum is one with meaning for all educators, but calls for special attention from those who look at the curriculum whole. Passow concluded that programs for the gifted and the deprived which have been conceived as part of an integrated, articulated, and sequential plan are more likely to have sustained educational impact than the patchwork tinkering that is more typical of many school programs.

These ideas are as relevant to teachers as to specialized curriculum workers. As indicated earlier in this paper, the teacher is the central figure utilizing ideas and materials in making decisions appropriate to individuals and groups within a complex setting. More than any other person, he is responsible for providing the range of learning opportunities needed in a given context and for assisting the pupil in selecting and making productive use of such opportunities. Ensuring continuity, sequence, articulation, and balance is a special responsibility of his. The chances that he will be able to discharge this responsibility well are, of course, enhanced or limited by expectancies set outside of his own frame of decision making.

With the increasing pattern of fragmentation in collegiate programs and the expectancy that teachers specialize in an individual discipline, it will become more important for some professional educators to be specialized generalists. These generalists will have a double-pronged specialty; they will be interdisciplinary specialists focusing their scholarship on the whole curriculum and its development. They will assume responsibility for working with future and beginning teachers to develop concepts of a total educational program in the elementary or secondary school. They will assist future teachers in relating the broad social goals of education to specifics of the curriculum and teaching. They will engage students in study of continuity, articulation, and balance in the curriculum. In performing these functions, they will be critical agents in the total education of future teachers who will be expected to make rational decisions in their own roles and in concert with their colleagues.

PRESENT OVEREMPHASES WILL MOVE TOWARD THE CENTER, AND BALANCE WILL BE ACHIEVED

One of the values of gaining historical perspective is the knowledge that checks and balances tend to operate in education, as in other realms of living and working. On this basis alone it can be predicted that the present overemphases in certain aspects of study and practice in education will be checked and new, more appropriate balance will be achieved.

Current concentration on the cognitive will be counteracted by renewed attention to the affective. Man is a feeling as well as a knowing being. Checks are already evident. Standards for admission to college that rely solely on the cognitive are recognized as inadequate; the point is even more sharp in admission to teacher education programs. Youth search for a reason for being, and they do not find it in pursuit of their academic subjects. People seek ways out of their loneliness, and the loneliness they feel is not at the cognitive level. If the peoples of the world are to have any peace and harmony, brotherly love is essential, and such love is not made of rational processes only.

Present imbalanced attention to the science of teaching and scientific study of teaching will find its rightful place in examination of the whole of teaching. Rumblings of dissatisfaction are getting louder all the time, dissatisfactions that are akin to fear—fear that teaching will be so dissected, so cold, so depersonalized, so dehumanized, so unimaginative that the creative mind, the warm person, the artist practitioner will be forever lost to the profession.

Another imbalance in the contemporary scene favors only that research which is experimental in design, which employs patterns of the physical sciences, and which lends itself to complicated statistical analysis. This kind of research will eventually take its rightful place alongside of other methods for discovering knowledge, for testing hunches, and for abstracting wisdom in educational practice. That this will happen is a foregone conclusion, because many of the most critical problems in curriculum and teaching cannot be studied in their natural context unless methods other than experimental research are employed.

At the Curriculum Conference two years ago, Alice Miel presented an analysis showing a pattern of emphasis and re-emphasis on major concerns in the curriculum and teaching field. The significant point of her analysis was that a re-emphasis on an aspect is always a new emphasis, always at a higher level of sophistication, always bringing to bear more knowledge. We may predict with considerable confidence that this will continue to happen, that as we return our attention to the affective domain, to the whole of teaching, and to a wider range of methods of research we will do so at a higher level of scholarship. It is quite likely that some educators will wish to return to where they were comfortably situated a few years ago and that others will overcompensate as a rebellion against the present, but scholars in education will take every possible advantage of keeping in balance attention to all facets of the field.

A MODIFIED CONCEPTION OF PRE-SERVICE
TEACHER EDUCATION WILL BE COMMON

The other day I was interviewed by a free-lance writer who is doing an article for *Good Housekeeping* on the assets and liabilities of the teacher tenure system as it operates today. His main question was, "How can a tenure system insure security for the competent teacher and at the same time guarantee that incompetent teachers will not be protected?" My response to this question was expression of opinion which I now suggest as prediction. Granting of tenure and license will be seen as a single process and will be based on demonstrated competence over a period of at least three years. Preparing institutions and school systems will be held accountable for recommending teachers for license-tenure. Rationale for this point of view was presented in 1959 in the report of the New Horizons Project. Since publication of that report, the idea of more systematically bridging the gap between pre- and in-service teacher education and the proposal that both schools and colleges assume responsibility for steps leading to licensure have received added impetus. Rivlin has suggested that "pre-tenure preparation" supplant pre-service preparation, not only in terminology but in concept. Conant has proposed postponement of licensure until a teacher's competence has been attested to by the school system. Internships, jointly planned and supervised by college and school personnel, are on the increase.

Our present conception of pre-service teacher education as a four- or five-year program at an institution of higher education is inadequate. It is apparent that we need to think of the education of a beginning teacher as starting with his admission to a collegiate program and extending formally to the granting of license and tenure. We are, then, talking about a six-, seven-, or eight-year program of preparation, in which both college and school personnel participate.

Institutions of Higher Education and Schools Will Join Forces in the Preparation of Teachers

That both college and school personnel will participate in the preparation of teachers is so important as to call for special comment. On the surface it may not seem to you to forecast much change in teacher education because school people are already involved. For the most part, however, their present involvement is a willingness of teachers to have student teachers in their classrooms and to carry out the functions set for them by college personnel. This situation is going to change to a marked degree. The pre-certification program that will extend into the first three years of teaching service will be a shared responsibility. Colleges will assume a major role for the early years of preparation, and responsibility will gradually shift to school personnel in later years, while college personnel continue to share in induction of the novice into the profession.

The exact nature of differentiation in this shared responsibility will be something like this: Colleges will assume charge of the liberal education and the subject-matter specializations of teachers. Both dimensions of preparation will extend through the first three years of teaching. Colleges will assume major responsibility for beginning study of education, but such study will be centered in educational laboratories—schools, particularly. Those who direct and guide this study will be members of college faculties, some of whom will have joint appointments in school systems, much the same as there are now joint appointments in subject-matter departments and departments of education in colleges.

A period of student teaching, under the guidance of a carefully selected teacher and adjusted to the ability of the student, will precede an internship, in which the beginning teacher will have the special help of both college and school personnel. During the next two years, schools and colleges in cooperation will make special provision for continuing education, including opportunities for beginning teachers to study teaching, class and school organization, politics, history, and philosophy of education, purposes, major questions on curriculum, and methods for discovery and verification of new knowledge in education. Colleges will offer courses, seminars, and independent study arrangements for beginning teachers to continue study in the liberal arts and to do advanced study in their subject-matter specialties. Those teachers who have demonstrated ability to teach, to keep on learning, and to abstract principles from their learning will be recommended for licensure and tenure by representative school and college persons working together in the collection and analysis of data used in making such recommendations.

TEACHERS WILL BE PROFESSIONAL SCHOLARS

What has been almost hollow verbiage in the past—that teachers should be scholars and professionals—will take on serious meaning in the future. Characteristics of current research efforts in education point to new responsibilities for teachers. Funds granted by both government and private enterprise go as readily to schools and school personnel as to colleges and universities. Research in education, sponsored by university personnel, tends to utilize schools and school populations as subjects. A predominant focus of many investigations is teaching behavior, and more and more teachers are called upon to participate responsibly in research. School systems, formerly limiting their studies to statistical data about their students, teachers, and communities, now begin to employ specialists in educational research to work with their staffs in systematic study of all parts of the educational program.

It seems clear that tomorrow's teacher will be central in the study of theory and practice in education. An expected part of the teacher's role will be his continuing study, not only of his subject-matter specialty, but also of his practice. He will initiate and conduct research himself and in concert with his peers. He will have released time and expert help in planning and conducting his study.

The predicted close relationships between school and college personnel during the first three years of teaching prior to granting of license and tenure will tend to continue throughout the career of the teacher. State certification will cease to be concerned with regulatory requirements for forcing continued study on the part of teachers. School systems will abandon practices of requiring courses and credits for salary increments. But teachers will be students more than they are at present. They will be scholars whose internal motivation impells them to take advantage of opportunities to improve. Their preparation will have set this pattern, and the environmental expectancies will make it desirable.

PROSPECTS FOR CURRICULUM CHANGE IN PUBLIC SCHOOLS

Joseph O. Loretan

It becomes disturbingly obvious to me, as I read through the current crop of scholarly papers and as I consider my own convictions regarding the prospects for curriculum change, that there are serious conflicts of ideas between the technologists and the humanists. I become concerned when I see school people seemingly failing in leadership at a point when education is changing into a more structured technology. If this change is to come about, I want to be sure the educators are calling the turns. I want assurance that the systems developed by the engineers are under the control of people with imagination and humanistic values—that is, the strong and fundamental conviction that people are more important than techniques and machines.

HUMANITY AND TECHNOLOGY

When the behavioral psychologists, led by Skinner, first began defining "learning" in terms of extremely small steps, we educators had to re-examine the structure of the disciplines and our methods of planning. For example, the other day I listened to a young man from Stanford addressing a group of educators on the subject of innovation. He told of a scheme whereby youngsters go through lessons using a typewriter and a programmed teaching machine; in a matter of minutes a computer, which is part of this programmed device, analyzes children's responses against information already

Joseph O. Loretan is Deputy Superintendent, Instruction and Curriculum, Board of Education of the City of New York.

stored in its memory, and prepares for the teacher an analysis of what the student has learned and what he should be learning. There seems no doubt that refinements of this type of programmed learning could be of considerable help to teachers and school administrators in achieving genuine individualized instruction. Leaders in education had better work diligently with the engineers in this brave new world of cybernetics.

Then, of course, I heard with some nostalgia and a great deal of interest the remarks of Hollis L. Caswell as he pointed out that the goals of education are derived from the values of society as they move into operational patterns through the curriculum specialists. I think we are all somewhat alarmed about the pace of change in education, the increasing amount of knowledge that is expected of us, and the enormous depth of the information expected of the classroom teacher and of the school supervisor.

There are major educational revisions going on in the nation today, and many of them are occurring in the great cities. There is even some movement on the part of educators in the great cities to begin exchanging ideas with each other. Today I am flying out to a meeting in California where the fifteen great cities will exchange views on a number of matters—textbooks, finance, and some aspects of communication and language arts as they affect the disadvantaged youngsters.

CONCERN FOR PLANNING

I think that I share Professor Caswell's concern for planning. Education is progressing, certainly, but are we educators *planning* as we advance? Sometimes the progress gets ahead of the planning, and therefore such meetings as this Curriculum Conference can have immense value for the participants in the area of planning. I speak as one personally involved in a dozen curriculum development plans; for example, I just did a survey of social science projects throughout the nation. Several worthwhile projects are developing in the Portland School System. There, a team of university professors, skillful in the design and development of curriculum, are involved with subject-matter specialists and school people to build a curriculum in a planned fashion.

Wisconsin is another state where there has been a broad-scale approach on a K-12 basis in history and the social sciences. They include all the disciplines—anthropology, political science, economics, and all of the others—but they do not treat them as individual disciplines, pure and separate. Rather, the disciplines are blended into an inter-disciplinary approach, so structured, that the particular emphasis of each social science discipline is taught in relationship to the others.

I think curriculum design has much to gain from such an eclectic approach, from seizing upon the important concepts—such as space and time —and really spelling them out for youngsters and for teachers. They need to understand the essence of space—have it clarified to include the area around a desk as well as the area in the sky. If they relate this concept of space to the areas charted on maps, these maps will become meaningful in understanding historical change and the impact of man's inventions upon his history. Curriculum change is not going to be easy to achieve through this type of integrated approach. However, thoughtful men, joining in teams and foregoing some of their separate concerns, can do a notable job in our time. In this respect, school administrators, generalists, and the faculties of teachers colleges can help by exercising leadership and bringing together people who may be warring among themselves.

SOME OBSTACLES TO PROGRESS

We have goals now that need to move forward constantly, that cannot be put aside if the nation is to remain strong and become stronger. We have, for example, the struggle in civil rights and civil liberties which cannot be resolved until enough minds change from a racist approach to a truly American one. All curriculum people—subject-matter specialists, generalists, methodologists, and scholars in universities—must join forces with those who understand group dynamics, so that, together, they can come forth with a strategy that will enable the nation, through the education of youngsters from the kindergarten through adulthood, to achieve an integrated society.

Integration is a paramount issue. What are the prospects for changes in this area? Certainly, changes are not going to be achieved without tremendous effort by all parties. The chief school officers of the nation are now fully aware of the significance of and requirements for these changes. The federal government has shown a resolution to take the necessary steps in what Gunnar Myrdal has so aptly called "the American dilemma." Thanks to recent legislation and judicial action, it has been put before the community as a dilemma that, if it is not resolved, can destroy this nation. How can we insist that everyone should have an equal opportunity while we drag our feet in furnishing the opportunities? This is a challenge that every teacher has to face every day, that the colleges must also face, and that the total community must be ready to face.

Regarding integration the prospects for change are probably better in the schools than in employment or other areas. One of our problems in the large urban centers is how to achieve integration of the schools in a way that will be as satisfactory to the community as to the school people. We do not want our neighbors in the community threatening to move out to the suburbs. However, these threats are being made, and they must be faced by all civic-minded people. Moving out of town is not the solution. It is not in the best interest of the nation. It is not going to be an easy problem to solve, but we cannot make it go away by running from it.

ARTICULATION AND MULTI-SENSORY LEARNING

There are two other general comments I want to make, before talking about New York City's efforts to develop concrete plans for teaching youngsters about the problems they will face as young men and women. First, it seems to me that one of the things we talk about fervently in curriculum development is articulation. We talk very, very fervently about continuous progress. We maintain grades and classification schemes in which children mark time. We talk about individualization but instruct on a mass basis.

My second concern is the fact that we educators have never agreed on how much time a particular learning should take, when it should be introduced, and to whom it should be taught. In this connection, it could be useful to consider how some of the nation's prominent educators view the fundamental goals of education.

Let us consider music for a moment. As a subject area, it may not be as important as mathematics and science in the minds of some people, and these people may wonder why I think it is as important and what it has to do with mastery at different age periods? However, just to give yourselves an idea of what the learning objectives are in music, consider the following: perform a musical piece, theme, or figure in any medium; read the standard musical notation scheme in its accompanying figures, numbers, and verbal symbols; listen to music with understanding and enjoyment; be knowledgeable about composers, performers, periods, styles, instruments, and works and about the place of music in western culture; seek musical experiences; develop preferences and make judgments about music and its performance; give minimum attention to opera, program music, non-western music, and knowledge about performers; and forget about "rock and roll" entirely.

I didn't make up the above list—I came across it down in Washington. I do not mean to debate the value of this set of objectives; I mentioned it only to demonstrate some of the problems involved in achieving proper scope, sequence, and balance in the curriculum and in deciding who studies what when.

The questions of curriculum design and development are going to continue to be difficult and troublesome. Marshall McLuhan, in his *Guten-*

berg Galaxy, talks about linear learning versus a more global, multi-sensory learning. From the increasing insights we are gaining from neurology, we know that the learning that is accomplished can be a function of further learning. Thus, the brain is in the process of generating itself and improving itself as a learning instrument while it is actively acquiring knowledge. An example of such linear learning is the skill of reading, which has been the mark of an educated man since the invention of the printing press and movable type. If, instead of considering linear learning as a model, we define it as a concept of education in which youngsters learn in several dimensions simultaneously, listening and observing in a global fashion, using oral-aural as well as visual senses, it seems that we have another new ingredient to ponder in planning for more effective teaching of youngsters.

Children receive a strong impact from this global type of learning, from eight to twelve hours a day, via their radios and television sets, from birth. Then they come to school, and we hand them a pre-primer or a readiness book, and we virtually forget all the valuable learning that has already taken place. Yet, in spite of the fact that this preschool experience demonstrates the fastest learning rate that children can achieve, we go right back to horse and buggy procedures in trying to teach everything in linear fashion. The ducks, quails, and dogs in suburbia, or similar nonurban scenes, puzzle city children, at a time when they are at a peak in terms of perceptions, impressions, and insights—even though they cannot yet verbalize them. We still treat multi-media types of learning as frills instead of recognizing them as, potentially, the essentials in education. Overhead projectors, pictorial materials, and programmed devices of all kinds ought to be useful and integral parts of the teacher's paraphernalia for effecting learning. These materials and equipment can be as easy to obtain and as useful and as essential a part of the plan as a piece of chalk. Until the schools ask for and receive them, we cannot suggest that we are making full use of all of the available teaching materials.

INNOVATION IN NEW YORK CITY

Now let us talk about New York City. Some of the projects now underway in New York have a bearing, I think, on the topic assigned to me for this address. Of these projects, the one with probably the greatest potential for real curriculum change is the project being carried on with Educational Testing Service. This effort was begun after we discontinued administering group intelligence tests in New York City because we found this test to be unreliable.

We are working on tools that will help the teachers study the behavioral clues that indicate intellectual growth. We are helping the teachers to begin studying these clues in the first grade. Next year, hopefully, we will include the kindergarten; the year after that, the pre-kindergarten; and, eventually, the second grade. What we are trying to achieve is real understanding on the part of the teachers of how to use behavioral clues that the children demonstrate—how to interpret those behavioral clues in terms of cognitive ability. For example, what does it indicate in terms of intellectual development when a child looks at a balance beam in which there are weights placed on either side and begins to move the weights in a way that indicates that he is grasping the fact that numbers have patterned relationships?

Behavioral clues to cognitive development

There are three parts to this project. The first part of the project required the production of a listing of behavioral clues to cognitive development which could be useful to teachers. The first-grade teachers from twenty-five experimental schools were involved in this project, in addition to a team of professors from Educational Testing Service, plus a group from New York City Board of Education headquarters. The teachers provided a list of all the behavioral manifestations that they felt indicated alertness or brightness or cognitive growth. For example, one teacher said that she had a six-year-old named Juan who made an abysmally low score on a prevailing readiness test—one she used regularly. She said that, so far as that test is concerned, he is a complete failure, yet he can take the appropriate amount of laundry across town on a bus, weigh out the laundry, count out the correct amount of money for the laundering, go back across town with the clean laundry, let himself into the house, put the clothes away in their proper drawers, leave and lock the house, and get to school on time. Is not this accomplishment an indication of intellectual capability, asks this teacher?

Culling the work of Piaget, Bruner, Guilford, and Torrance, we made a second list of items considered by them to be evidence of intellectual growth in terms of specified behaviors. These are behaviors which indicate an understanding of quantitative relationships and show the type of logical thinking needed in making inferences. The first list, provided by the teachers on the basis of the year's observation in the schools, used as a guide various questions and proposals made by the investigating group. Then we merged the two lists; in the synthesis that resulted, there was a very high correlation between behaviors chosen by seasoned, experienced teachers as indicators of the intellectual ability of youngsters and those selected by the professors and, from the works of Piaget, Bruner, and the others. The next step was the preparation of a book entitled *Let's Look at First Graders,* which was distributed to all the first-grade teachers involved in the project. We now have four districts trying out this program. In addition to the book, *Let's Look at First Graders,* in which all these different types of activities and different behavioral manifestations are described in relation to behavioral clues, we have given them another booklet entitled *From Theory to Classroom.*

TEACHING FOR COGNITIVE GROWTH

Part two of this project concerns the ongoing curriculum activities. This project has important implications for curriculum, because, obviously, what you teach a youngster is determined by what you know about his intellectual development. In the past we have virtually prevented the teachers from forming their own judgment of such development by dictating to them the various points at which the student is able to progress. For example, we say: "In the fourth month you can start on reading instruction," and so on.

Having, as I mentioned earlier, discarded the group IQ tests, we decided to substitute achievement tests, to be administered at various points along the way, because these tests do not attack the personality of the child from the point of view of predestination. Achievement tests can tell a child, "Well, all right, you didn't do well this time, but, if you exert yourself and we help you, you ought to be able to do better on this test next time." This is better than saying, as the group IQ test does: "You're a nice, mediocre kid; just don't strain yourself." So many guidance counselors say to so many parents: "Don't push him." I certainly do not believe in "pushing" at the wrong time, but neither do I believe that a little magic number, derived once or twice or three times in the life of a child, can honestly determine whether the child can grow intellectually or not. Thus, the second step in our project was to concede that some youngsters are not stimulated, are not attracted, are not moved by the routine work that goes on. Therefore, we encouraged the teachers to observe each youngster in play, in his routine classroom activities, and in chores he performs, in hopes that the teachers would come to see that some youngsters are not stimulated in school because the transition from their homes to a conventional curriculum may be impossible for them. These children, in their homes, may have been on a different wavelength entirely—not a worse wavelength, simply a different one. To help the teachers in the project work with these youngsters, we have developed a number of tasks that we call "developmental" tasks—extra, different, ingenious tasks. The teachers try these out on the youngsters—different types of games, attractive puzzles of different kinds, picture cards of all kinds, all of the paraphernalia of an attractive, challenging kind of program for youngsters. By observing the youngsters at these tasks, and using the behavioral clues, the teacher can learn about each particular child. She can derive notions about each child's degree of ability to learn generalizations and abstractions. She can do these things, once she knows what the behavioral clues are and what kind of tasks he can or cannot perform.

EVALUATION OF COGNITIVE GROWTH

Then, there is a third part of the project—evaluation of the child's learning. In this process, we use all the various techniques and behavioral clues collected previously to find out if the youngster has learned or is challenged to learn the concepts we are attempting to get across to him. We assess his progress to find out, for example, whether this youngster understands quantitative relationships. Does he understand that if you transfer a bit of water from a jug into a narrow, thin test tube, and then to a flat receptacle, such as a soup plate, you still have the same amount of water? The probing is aimed at evaluating the child's conceptual understanding of differences, of class groups, of types, of sets. We then assess these understandings in terms of what teachers would normally call a test, asking children twelve or fifteen questions, such as: "What does this look like?" Such questions have long been part of many of the traditional readiness materials, but, in this particular type of curriculum and instructional approach, they serve a different purpose. Here, the assessment is a by-product; it is a diagnostic tool used to help the teacher chart the direction of her teaching, and see where reinforcement or improvement is needed.

After making the assessment, after having analyzed the child's understandings, do we score him? We do not. We simply try again, using the same concepts with new types of materials—new and different and various types of materials, but the same concept. If it was oranges and apples that we were working with before, to instill the concept of classification, we try pears and bananas the next time. And then, after a day or a week of trying the new methods, we give him another test, one that uses a whole new set of objects and materials; we even put the test on different colored paper. This way, we find out whether any progress has been made as a result of our changed techniques. Again, at the end of that second assessment, we do not grade the child. We do not do it even after the third assessment. On the fourth and fifth occasion we record two tentative marks, one on the degree of achievement that is evidenced and the other on the rate of learning that has occurred between the first assessment and the most recent one.

Most of the "general intelligence" tests make a fatal assumption—one that must have been worked out many many years ago in a nice, small, very homogeneous town. The assumption made by most of these tests is that all the youngsters have had common experiences. We do not make that assumption in our testing; we provide the common experience. We provide it in the instructional program, so that what we are diagnosing is the real effectiveness of the teaching as well as the ability of the youngster. Because we are working with concepts, generalizations, and abstractions, we are building intellectual power. I think the potential of this project is enormous. I think that, if we do this in the pre-kindergarten and the kindergarten, we should find, by the end of the second grade, that we have not only stimulated intellectual growth, but we have also found out a great deal more about how each youngster is functioning.

SOCIAL SCIENCE PROJECTS

We have a number of new projects in history and the social sciences. To begin with, we do not say "social studies," you notice, and that causes some pain. We insist on saying history and the social sciences, although, of course, nearly all studies are social studies. We wanted to have much of this particular learning area understood structurally so we didn't bother with the debate that has been raging all over the country about whether to approach this in a disciplinary or an interdisciplinary manner. We argue that you need both approaches. Maybe that is a compromise. We argue that, from the time they begin in kindergarten, youngsters are capable of some understanding of the structure of a subject, provided the material is presented in the language of children.

If the learning theorists are right about the amount of learning that little children can achieve, and if the increase in knowledge is going to continue at its present pace as man learns more about himself, about his society, and about his world and other worlds, then we have excellent motivation to begin earlier to educate our children and to simplify the basic concepts of knowledge for them. We have already done some experimental teaching of economic concepts in the first grade. Hard-boiled school superintendents, principals, and teachers in the one hundred schools involved have arrived at the stage where they are insulted if they do not receive extra money to buy the new, attractive materials of the type that can help first-grade children understand and talk about the concepts of producing services or goods, making investments, or supply and demand. How deeply this will affect children's insights when they grow into adulthood, you and I will never find out. Some younger members of this group may be around long enough to decide that this was just another one of the dreams of some professor and some superintendent. But I for one, although I did not create this idea, have studied it and am impressed with it.

Based upon our research, we found that little children have great interest in politics and can grasp many ideas about politics and government and power and power figures. This is true as early as the first and second grade. Notions about time, one of the most difficult things to teach, change if the method is changed. The youngsters who watch a worm travel across a blotter and ascertain how long it takes the worm to get across are studying time. Recently, we used a cartoon to help children understand them. It was a sequence about bubble gum—four pictures: one in which the bubble had just burst, and one in which the bubble was expanding, and one in which the bubbles were of different types and sizes including one at the earliest stage of growth. Could the children sort out the chronological sequence and place the bursting bubble in its proper place in the sequence? Yes, they could. First-grade pupils could do it. We are doing the same thing with all the other subjects—taking generalizations and experimenting to find out what sort of material we need to develop, how to make it understood by youngsters, and in what manner we should approach it.

This is a bit of the history of New York City's social science program, which will eventually cover kindergarten up through the twelfth grade. It may take five years to complete the task—two years have already been spent. We have access to the best ideas and materials in the country, some of which are extraordinarily good. We have investigated the Wisconsin Project, mentioned earlier, which has developed a scope and sequence of political science and anthropology and the other disciplines on a K-12 basis. I have also discussed Portland's work in this area. Bruner, Patterson, and Morison, of Educational Services Incorporated, have been developing material that we are experimenting with in New York. I think we convinced them that just trying these things out in Newton, a nice, little, comfortable, suburban town, would not offer a challenge worthy of professors. Instead of allowing our professors to remain in ivory towers, we ought to invite them to bring the ideas they have developed in their universities and the colleges into the city school systems. Universities and colleges can be extremely conservative, and few professors have spent enough time in urban schools to really know what they are all about.

TEAM TEACHING IN HIGH SCHOOL

We have also developed a correlated curriculum for the high schools. We have achieved some team teaching in academic high schools where nobody thought it could happen. The teachers—an English teacher, a science teacher, a math teacher, and an industrial arts teacher—teamed up to write a curriculum, based on technology, for selected youngsters. They worked as a team to teach those youngsters, and the teaching is sticking. The students in their classes are staying in school, instead of joining the dropouts.

In discussing these new curriculum thrusts in New York City, I would be unrealistic, and somewhat dishonest in speaking with a group like this, if I were to suggest that our implementation matched our inclinations. It is a long, bumpy, and sometimes nonexistent road that leads from theory to classroom.

The discussion of how to affect change has been going on for at least as many years as I have been an educator. Now I think the time has come when we must address ourselves to the need for change among those who have been discussing how to affect change, because—we must face it— little has happened as a result of these deliberations. It is still our major problem in education, and, until we resolve the problem of how to move from dream to reality, we have not exercised our responsibility as practicing educators.

CURRICULUM AS
A FIELD OF STUDY

Dwayne Huebner

I SHOULD LIKE to offer four propositions, upon which this discussion of curriculum will be based:

1. Current conceptions of curriculum are inadequate, in that they tie the educative process only to the world of man's technique, and exclude ties to the world of his spirit.

2. This inadequacy stems from an overdependency upon a conception of value as goals or objectives, and a consequent overdependency upon learning as the major characteristic of man's temporality.

3. This inadequacy can be partially corrected by a conception of curriculum as the design of an educative environment in which valued educational activity can occur.

4. This designing is inherently a political process by means of which the curricular worker seeks to attain a just environment.

In 1832 Oswald Spengler's pessimistic *Man and Technic* was published in English. He argued that man's Viking quality, his search for power, has resulted in the establishment of a machine technic which is in the process of destroying man, and that it is now beyond man's power to alter this destiny. He states:

> The lord of the World is becoming the slave of the Machine, which is forcing him—forcing us all whether we are aware of it or not—to follow its course. . . .
>
> All things organic are dying in the grip of organization. An artificial world is permeating and poisoning the natural. . . .

DWAYNE HUEBNER is Associate Professor of Education at Teachers College, Columbia University.

The history of this technics is fast drawing to its inevitable close. . . . Faced as we are with this destiny, there is only one world-outlook that is worthy of us, that which has already been mentioned as the choice of Achilles—better a short life, full of deeds and glory, than a long life without content. Already the danger is so great, for every individual, every class, every people, that to cherish any illusion whatever is deplorable . . . . Only dreamers believe that there is a way out. Optimism is cowardice.[1]

In 1964 Jacques Ellul's *The Technological Society*,[2] originally published in the 1950's in France, was translated into English. Ellul spelled out the danger more incisively. He defined technique not simply as machine, but as "the totality of methods rationally arrived at and having absolute efficiency (for a given stage of development) in every field of human endeavor." Technique permeates not simply the machine world, but the economic, political, and social structures of man's world. He points out that the two most commonly accepted characteristics of technique are its rationality and artificiality. But more significant are five other characteristics less widely acknowledged. First, its automatism:

> When everything has been measured and calculated mathematically so that the method which has been decided upon is satisfactory from the rational point of view, and when, from the practical point of view, the method is manifestly the most efficient of all those hitherto employed or those in competition with it, then the movement becomes self directing . . . . [Then] man is stripped of his faculty of choice and he is satisfied.[3]

Second, its self augmentation, the "automatic growth of everything which concerns technique." Here man has lost control of the growth of technique, as Spengler pointed out, or as McLuhan writes, "Man becomes, as it were, the sex organs of the machine."[4] Ellul states that "technical progress is irreversible" and that it tends to a geometric, not an arithmetic progression. It poses primarily technical problems which can only be resolved by technique and thus becomes a closed world.

Its third characteristic is its monism. "The technical phenomena, embracing all separate techniques forms a whole." Its fourth is its universalism; it "cannot be otherwise than totalitarian," and it "has taken over the whole of civilization." Technique tends to expand geographically, into all parts of the world; and qualitatively, into all of men's endeavors.

---

1 Oswald Spengler, *Man and Technic*, translated by Charles Francis Atkinson (New York: Alfred A. Knopf, 1932), pp. 90–104.

2 Jacques Ellul, *The Technological Society*, translated by John Wilkinson (New York: Alfred A. Knopf, 1964).

3 *Ibid.*, pp. 79–82.

4 Marshall McLuhan, *Understanding Media: The Extensions of Man* (New York: McGraw-Hill, 1964), p. 46.

Finally, technique is autonomous, a closed system, an end in itself. "The complete separation of the goal from the mechanism, the limitation of the problem to the means, and the refusal to interfere in any way with efficiency," all of this "lies at the basis of technical autonomy."

Ellul, in the book just mentioned, seems to share Spengler's pessimism. However, in a more recent article he suggests conditions which might lead to a solution of the problems posed by the autonomy of techniques.[5] It is relatively easy to hypothesize that the recent concern for instructional technology or instructional systems is but the result of technique's universalism reaching into the world of the school. This would, however, be mis-stating the case. For one thing such a view lends itself to a rejection of modern technologies in schools, as if the classroom were the last bastion of naturalness and humanness and consequently must be protected from the encroachments of this monster, technique. In fact, it would seem that technical developments point to what man is and what he can be as much as the arts. Whether we like what is pointed out is another question. To reject technological developments in classrooms is to reject part of man and to deny the evolution of new possibilities in man. If there is any place in our society where the struggle between the world of man's technique and the world of man's spirit should occur, it is the classroom. It is here that men should discover how to make technique serve man rather than man serve technique. It is in the classroom where the neotechnic civilization that Mumford[6] talks about should be aborning, for where else should man's spirit be uppermost?

The other things wrong with the hypothesis are that the universalism of technique first touched schools when the clock (which Mumford claims is the first technical development) was installed on the classroom wall; that technique achieved a firmer grip when the first mass medium, the book, was used; and that education really embraced technique when it became concerned about efficiency before the 1920's.[7]

The invasion of the schools by technique is not symbolized by modern developments in electronic instructional technology. Technique is already firmly, although perhaps not permanently, institutionalized in the means-ends language which guides the educational process. What is the first great question which focuses most of the debate in education? "What is the role

[5] Jacques Ellul, "The Technological Order," in Carl F. Stover (Ed.), *The Technological Order* (Detroit: Wayne State University Press, 1963), pp. 10–37. (This is a resumé of Ellul's earlier book.)

[6] Lewis Mumford, *Technique and Civilization* (New York: Harcourt, Brace and World, 1934).

[7] Lee Raymond Callahan, *Education and the Cult of Efficiency* (Chicago: The University of Chicago Press, 1962).

of the school?" or "What are the purposes of education?" What question do we try to get beginning teachers to ask as they plan? "What are your purposes?" "What are you trying to achieve?" "What is it that you want students to learn?" And the next question, which presumably can be answered only after the first—"How should the school be organized to achieve that end?" "How should your content and instruction be structured to get there?" Left unsung, but nevertheless in the back of everyone's mind is the criterion of efficiency. Whatever and however you organize, do so efficiently. Conceived that way, the machines and the new technologies are merely more efficient ways to reach goals. This is unfortunate. New educational technologies do increase educational efficiency through their quality as means. But new developments in educational media also suggest new values that could be achieved through education. This value-creating quality is hidden when new media are seen simply as means to ends.

Most educators seem unaware of their involvement with and commitment and subservience to the self-augmenting technological order. Their curriculum language hides this reality from them. In fact, it also hides how new technologies could be used to sharpen the struggle between man's techniques and man's spirit. The unfortunate equating of education with learning has pushed into ascendancy theories of learning[8] and has justified the means-ends value system which is characteristic of technique. Focusing on learning as the primary working concept in curriculum will naturally push the educator to ask, "Well, what are they supposed to learn?" When these goals or expected outcomes are specified, then the learning theory supposedly tells the teacher how to use materials and what to do. The search is for the most effective means to realize the ends. Hence curriculum people search for the best materials, the most efficient organization, and the best grouping of children. Let me remind you again of Ellul's definition of technique: "The totality of methods rationally arrived at and having absolute efficiency (for a given stage of development) in every field of human endeavor." Learning theory is, thus, the handmaiden of technique in the schools. It subjects teacher, materials, and organization to the system. Theoretically, it prescribes the means and tells teachers and students how to act.

Do not misunderstand me, I am not against learning theories. As a language system in psychology, they exhibit man's transcendent spirit, his ability to reach out into the unknown. They are essential for the evolution of education. One of the major contributions of learning theory to education is to facilitate the construction of the educational environment. In

[8] For another criticism of the dominance of education by psychology see Joseph J. Schwab, "On the Corruption of Education by Psychology," *The School Review*, 67, Summer, 1958, pp. 169–184.

one sense, it might be said that learning theory has finally found its limited and proper place in curriculum as it makes possible teaching machines, programmed learning, and electronic, responsive environments such as that of Omar K. Moore.[9] Through the insights of reinforcement theory, those miserable old workbooks are being improved and may yet become functional in schools. Furthermore, through the development of many such environmental objects, the teacher is becoming a free agent again, for one of the characteristics of the older classroom technologies was that teachers became extensions of the technique. Builders of textbook series would describe in detail how a teacher should use the textbook. In effect, they were saying, "Here is the reality, the book. Now your role, teacher, is to become the active ingredient in this technology. How you feel is unimportant, for you are but an extension of the book and its purposes." The moment there is more than one technique available for the classroom, the teacher enters the realm of freedom and awesome choice. However, to the extent that learning theories become the sole sources of the educator's ideology, they bind the educational process into the technical order.

The problem, if not caused by the equating of education and learning, is at least epitomized by it. The difficulty is that man's spirit is much more complicated than we seem willing to believe. Oversimplified educational ideologies foster this misconception. The goal-oriented, person-shaping ideology of curriculum implies that youngsters can be molded to reach predetermined behaviors. The educational process is more complicated than that. The act of education is an act of human influence—or of "initiation," as Peters would say[10]—and there is nothing more complicated or awesome. The school is the meeting ground of a man becoming aware that he has a destiny and a social group seeking to determine that destiny. It is this idea of destiny that curriculum thought has destroyed by making learning the most important single concept in its language repertoire. In a sense, destiny has been replaced by destination, and learning has become the only valued form of living in school.

Man's nature is given by his temporality—the fact that he lives in time as well as in space. If this age of rapid change has done nothing else, it has disclosed that man is the being capable of continual modification and change. When the world was rather stable, at least over a twenty- or

[9] For the promises of learning theory in the design of the educational environment, see Robert Glaser (Ed.), *Teaching Machines and Programmed Learning, II, Data and Directions* (Washington: Department of Audio-Visual Instruction, National Education Association, 1965).

[10] R. S. Peters, "Education as Initiation," in Reginald D. Archimbault (Ed.), *Psychological Analysis and Education* (London: Routledge and Kegan Paul, 1965), pp. 87–111.

thirty-year period, the educator could well envision a state of man with more or less permanent and fixed characteristics. He could imagine a perfect gentleman, an ideal citizen, or a skilled artisan, and he could program a curriculum accordingly. Today this is impossible, for change outside of man is too rapid. This is exciting and revealing, for it points so clearly to the fact that man is embodied change. Not only can he produce change, but he himself is capable of continual change. To be a man is to be capable of finite change and evolution until death. Indeed, the insight of the existentialists seems relevant, that man's biography may be written, his project complete, only after he is dead. A living man may always become something else; if he doesn't of his own accord, the world may push him into it. How do we deal with this in education? The standard answer is, "by helping people learn how to learn." I think this answer is inadequate, for it hides the question or the problem within existing categories; whereas the existing categories need to be upset, maybe even destroyed, so new questions and problems can emerge. Rather, it seems that this awareness of the significance of change deals the death blow to the concept of learning as central in curriculum thought. It is still necessary, for it is an instrumental category for fabricating an educational environment. But I do not believe that it can continue to be the central category of curriculum thought. Learning is an attachment, a fixation, a state of conditionedness; while man's essence is given by the antinomies of attachment and detachment, fixation and freedom, conditionedness and unconditionedness. Learning implies a determining of behavior, while man's reactions in the world are partially indeterminate. Learning implies a destination; whereas living as a man implies a destiny. In some ways the discussions about creativity a few years ago pointed to this conflict, for the educator, between the determinateness of learned behavior and the freedom essential for creative behavior. And, of course, one is not possible without the other. But when learning remains the central concept in curriculum, we tend to focus on only one side of man's ambiguous situation in this world.

The basic problem is finding a way to conceptualize man's durational quality—the fact that man's existence is a temporal existence. It has continuity, it extends into the past and into the future. It could almost be said that man is a "human becoming" rather than a human being, but to say so is to throw overboard the philosophical heritage which deals with the nature of being. It might be said that man's home is not space but time (hence the significance of history as the foundation of all realms of life and knowledge). The educator has had difficulty dealing with the temporal quality of man, which is one of the reasons he has latched onto the behavioral scientist's notions of learning and goal or objective. To conceive of behavior as goal-oriented is to bring to one level of awareness this durational quality. Learning is that process which occurs between the identification and the attainment of the goal. The problem arises when there is no goal. What happens then? Does life have no durational quality? Unfortunately one branch of the publishing field has destroyed the significance of the words, but time is life and vice-versa. To waste time is not to waste a commodity, it is to waste one's life. To kill time is to say that life during those moments is of no significance and that the person might as well be dead. Time wasted in classrooms is an almost unforgivable crime because it is life and the precious eternal moment that are really being wasted.

But the behavioral scientist, upon whom the educator has become too dependent, has trouble dealing with the temporal qualities of existence. He tends to spatialize life, to assume that time as a dimension has the same qualities as space, and to forget the irreversibility and unpredictable qualities of man's temporality. Hannah Arendt indicates that these qualities require the power to forgive and to promise in social life.[11] Developmental psychologists, such as Gesell, introduce the notion of stage; the person jumps from stage to stage. An observer readily sees the stages but has difficulty seeing the process of movement between stages. The curriculum worker has the same difficulty. He identifies concepts or attitudes or skills that are to be developed, and the student goes from one level of skill or concept to another. Again, then, the time in-between is conceptualized as learning. The curriculum specialist has trouble thinking of the in-between times as life with inherent value—these times are simply pathways to ends. Of course, the curriculum worker and his cohort, the behavioral scientist, have tried to get away from this by discussion of processes: the knowledge-making process, the problem-solving process, the discovery process, and the creative process. But each of these also has an end which is used to identify the consequences of the process. It is unfortunate that the educator has neglected other fields of insight, for the philosopher, the artist, and the theologian all have dealt with man as a temporal being.[12]

Closely related to this conceptual problem of dealing with man's temporality is the problem of value in curriculum. The educator's major approach to value is that of an end to be achieved, an instrumental type of

[11] Hannah Arendt, *The Human Condition* (Chicago: University of Chicago Press, 1958).

[12] Henri Bergson, *An Introduction to Metaphysics*, translated by T. E. Helmo (New York: Liberal Arts Press, 1949); Martin Heidegger, *Being and Time*, translated by John Macquerrie and Edward Robinson (New York: Harper and Row, 1962); Joseph Campbell (Ed.), *Man and Time*, papers from the Erenos Yearbooks (Baltimore: The Johns Hopkins Press, 1956).

valuing. Constantly the questions are asked, "What are we trying to achieve?" "What are the goals of education?" "What is our purpose?" "How well will this device or textbook series accomplish our goals?" The problem of value is the most significant one faced by the curriculum worker. Unfortunately, most discussions of the problem are subsumed under this heading of purpose or objectives. The problem of value is closely tied to the processes of criticism. It is frequently through acts of criticism that implicit values are made explicit (art criticism) or that the need for new values is realized (social criticism). The major source of educational criticism internal to the educational process is evaluation. Almost the sole criterion for measuring the value of a school or curriculum is "How well were the goals achieved?" As the conceptual model of learning is thought by some to provide a model for teaching, so the conceptual model for evaluation is thought by most to be the model for curriculum planning. The existing model for evaluation, technically conceived, is fine and very productive. As a model for curriculum, the evaluation model is inadequate. Furthermore, evaluation is not the only form of valuing which may be brought to bear on educational processes. It could well be that the failure to provide other valuing procedures, or preferably, other forms of criticism, has led to the desire for a national testing program. It is so easy to criticize on the basis of ends achieved or not achieved, for this requires no discipline except for the instrument maker. To use other forms of criticism in the search for other values requires much more skill and knowledge.

Let me recapitulate the discussion so far. I have proposed that current ways of thinking about curriculum are inadequate because they tie the teacher and the student to the self-augmenting world of technique. This invasion of the schools by technique is not the result of our use of new instruments or technologies of instruction, but a result of our basic means-ends approach to education. This means-ends approach is typified most directly by our uncritical acceptance of learning as our key working concept, and by the conception of value as an end state to be reached. As long as educational values are conceptualized only as goals to be reached or behaviors to be learned, the classrooms will continue to serve man's technique rather than man's spirit.

If the means-ends model, goals to be achieved and learning theory as the way, is relegated to a subordinate position in curricular thought, then how can the curriclum specialist proceed?[13] First, he needs a way of

<hr>

[13] See R. S. Peters, *op. cit.*, and R. S. Peters, *Authority, Responsibility, and Education* (London: Allen and Unwin, 1962), chapter 7, "Must an Education Have an Aim?". For earlier attempts to deal with this problem, see Dwayne Huebner, "Moral Perspectives and the Curriculum" in Millard Clements and James B. Macdonald

thinking about man's existence in time and the phenomenon of change. If all of man's behavior in the educative process need not be conceptualized as learning, how else may it be designated? This becomes the problem of finding a way to talk about educational activity, for it is educational activity which must be uppermost in our thinking, not simply learning activity. The central notion for the curriculum specialist must be that of educational activity, a term which curriculum inquiry could fill with meaning. Next, the curriculum specialist needs a conception of value. Ends or objectives are obviously one form of value; technical in nature, but essential and legitimate in human affairs. However, technical valuing—that is, designating end states—is not the only form of valuing which must be brought to bear on educational activity. Once the notion of learning is relegated to a more appropriate place in curricular thought, then other forms of value assume a more important role. If determining and realizing value is an essential aspect of curricular thought, then its counterpart must also be accepted. Value tends to remain hidden and obscure unless the activity of criticism is also engaged in. Valuing and criticizing are two sides of the same coin, and both are essential activities within curricular endeavors. Finally, with ways to think about educational activity and its durational nature, and systems of valuing, then the curriculum specialist becomes a designer of an educative environment. Through his actions, his fabricating, he constructs an environment within which the student may live in educationally valuable ways. These seem to be some of the conceptual problems facing the student of the curriculum field today. The remainder of this paper will be concerned with some tentative directions for dealing with these problems.

In psychology, man's temporal nature is reflected in the concept of motivation and learning. The question asked is what pushes man ahead. The question assumes, it seems to me, a pre-twentieth century view of man in which stability was the reality and change the problem. Today change is the reality and stability is the problem. Assuming that man's life is given by his existence in time and change, the question which should be asked is what holds man back from realizing his man-nature, his continual capacity for personal evolution and change. The focus of search is not, then, what makes man grow and learn, or evolve; but rather what keeps him from so doing, what are the barriers in his way? Earlier, necessity was

---

(Eds.), *Moral Dilemmas of Public Schools* (Columbus, Ohio: Charles E. Merrill Books, in press). See also Dwayne Huebner, "Curricular Language and Classroom Meaning," paper delivered at the Research Institute of the Association for Supervision and Curriculum Improvement, Miami, 1965 and to be published in James B. Macdonald (Ed.), *Language and Meaning* (Washington: The Association, in press).

the prod, or, as folklore phrases it, "Necessity is the mother of invention." Today necessity is being taken care of by technique, which is self-augmenting. So necessity now serves the cause of technique, and in fact, technique establishes new necessities for men.[14] Necessity no longer gives man the nudge down his temporal path. I suggest that there are three factors which serve man's transcendence. The first two, which are interrelated, are language and social encounter. The third is man's capacity for wonder and awe.

Heidegger states that language is the " 'house of being' in which man lives."[15] Through language man participates in the conditioned and the unconditioned. On the one hand, language ties him to the world of necessity and technique, by giving him categories for getting around in this world. Language is the key to the puzzling world constructed by his fellow man. Without it, he cannot be a part of this world. On the other hand, language is the instrument of his freedom, the gift which can untie him, temporarily, from his world. It enables him to dream and to see possibilities not yet realized in his life or in his world. It enables him to be aware of values that might be manifest at a later time. Without language he cannot be apart from this world. Because language grows and emerges, men can grow and emerge. The two major vehicles of transcendence found in language are science and poetry.[16] In both, man reaches beyond himself through language. Through both, he contributes to the evolving of others by making new language patterns available. By means of both, he can become aware of what is yet hidden in his world of possibility. Both science and poetry are imaginative disciplines, in which the imagination is tested by appropriate forms of criticism. The dreams of science are criticized by empirical tests and by determining their congruity with other scientific statements. The dreams of poetry are tested by forms of aesthetic criticism, through which value is acknowledged and congruity with other aesthetic forms is determined. The critical act, whether the empirical test or the critical analysis, is the counterthrust which serves to support and to point out weaknesses, and to push the language creator into new realms of

14 See Hannah Arendt, *op. cit.*, chapters III and IV.

15 James M. Robinson and John B. Cobb, Jr. (Eds.), *The Later Heidegger and Theology*, Vol. I: New Frontiers in Theology (New York: Harper and Row, 1963), p. 45.

16 See John Macmurray, *Reason and Emotion* (New York: Barnes and Noble, 1962); Martin Heidegger, "Holderlin and the Essence of Poetry," in Heidegger, *Existence and Being* (Chicago: Henry Regnery, 1949); R. C. H. Siu, *The Tao of Science* (New York: John Wiley and Sons and the Technology Press, Massachusetts Institute of Technology, 1957); Walker Gibson (Ed.), *The Limits of Language* (New York: Hill and Wang, 1962); James B. Conant, *On Understanding Science* (New Haven, Conn.: Yale University Press, 1947).

being. Hopefully, the imaginative scientist or poet has built into his own working ways some of the appropriate critical methods, but if not, the larger social order provides the necessary criticism. To be introduced into the discipline of science or poetry is to be placed in one of man's temporal pathways, which has boundaries but no fixed ends. The scientist seeks to disprove his theories and to find new ways to express the characteristics of the world as he meets it. To be content with existing theories or existing ways of explaining the phenomena of the world is to give up the concern for scientific language. Likewise, the poet is never content with prior expressions of his awareness and values. He, too, seeks new language forms which enliven his participation in the world. To use dead language expressions is to be overcome by the inertia of the world as known; but to seek to keep language vital and alive is to contribute to the creation of the world. The joy and the power of language is not that it enables man to fit into the world, but that it leads man beyond the world as presently operating and into a tomorrow which may be better, more beautiful, and more in harmony with the human spirit.

Man's confrontation with man is also a vehicle of transcendence[17]— through conversation, argument, love, economic conflict, and cooperation, even war and hate, and simply by comparison. To be face to face with a man who speaks differently, wants other things, has other ways of life, or who sees the world differently is to be confronted with the inherent questions: "Who am I?" "Who is he?" and "Why are we the way we are?" If the questions are not dealt with honestly and openly, then they are eventually forced upon the confronters by conflict of interest, as is happening today in the integration battles, and the political and economic conflicts in our world. Inherent in each human confrontation is the possibility of growth and transcendence, for as man meets man, he meets the other: someone who differs and consequently someone who manifests other qualities of life and human value. The thinking, feeling, and seeing of others points to the way that I think, feel, and see, and suggests that the world that I think is out there is not the same world that the other thinks is out there. The inherent tension which exists between people because they do differ is, or can be, the source of new life and possibility. The question that must be asked is not "How can man learn to make social encounters vehicles of human transcendence?" but "What are the barriers in today's conditioned world, in the world of technique and necessity, which prevent man's realization of his temporal nature?"

Finally, man's capacity for wonder and awe is a potential vehicle for tran-

[17] Martin Buber, *I and Thou,* translated by Ronald Gregor Smith (New York· Charles Scribner's Sons, 1937).

scendence or temporal movement. Awe and wonder point to a world beyond man's ken, a world which invites his involvement at ever new levels of
existence. Science, art, and religion can all be instrumentalities to this awe
and wonder, but the confrontation of men with the non-man made is its
source. Man-made things and man-made customs constantly put before us
conditioned man and his trappings. To have man-made things and conventions stripped away by a new scientific discovery, a new technological invention, or a new art work, thus suddenly uncovering or discovering that which
was there all the time, is awe producing. The moment of awe is the moment of humility, when one becomes aware of what one is and is not. To
paraphrase Abraham J. Heschel, wonder is the beginning of awe, awe is the
beginning of wisdom.[18]

The significance of science is not simply that we understand the world
and the tools for its use, but that the world becomes a response-world, as
witness the notion of anti-matter or the DNA molecule. The significance of
art is not that beauty is produced, but that our eyes are opened to see differently. The significance of technique is not that necessity is cared for, but
that our senses are extended—witness the awesome microscopic world and
the world under the sea. To have frequent confrontations between man
and the awe-producing world of not-man is to again start one on the road
of his temporality and change. For through this moment of awe or wonder,
the individual can realize how inadequate his existing ways of behavior and
thinking are; he recognizes how much of the world escapes his grasp, and
how much there is yet to be known or valued or experienced. Why is it,
then, that the confrontation between man and not-man does not always result in transcendence and growth? Probably not because man has not
learned to respond, but because the world of awe and wonder has been hidden by necessity, technique, and truthless language. Perhaps it is better to
remain speechless, awed, with a child who is overcome by a sunset than to
say "How beautiful," thus labeling and reducing to trite words an experience which transcends words and men.

Man's temporal quality, his life in time, is partially assured if language,
human encounter, and the encounter with the awesome world of the non-
man made are seen, not as aspects of necessity, but as the life-giving sources
of man's spirit. Man's participation in this ambiguous world of necessity
and freedom, or of the conditioned and the unconditioned, is characterized
by his use of language, his meetings with others, and his encounters with
the non-man-made world. Language is a token of man's necessity, a key
element in his technique. But it is also his major vehicle of freedom of his

[18] Abraham J. Heschel, *God in Search of Man: A Philosophy of Judaism* (New
York: Farrar, Strauss, 1955).

spirit, his most powerful way of escaping the clutches of technique. The social encounter with others is necessary in this complex social and economic world, and social ways are conditioned. But social encounters can be pathways to a future which can emerge. The meeting of man with not-man may be seen as man using the world or gaining mastery over it by technique. But it is also a source of joy and freedom, an invitation to growth and evolution if man can stay open and receptive to it. These, then, are some ways of talking about human movement through time. The possible emergence of man can be seen as he uses language, meets others, and confronts the world. The emergent or transcending participation in language, social encounter, or the non-man-made world could be dimensions of educational activity.

The problem of value is a tricky ethical and axiological one. I cannot hope to deal with it, nor am I capable of doing so. It seems to me that one of its most personal manifestations is the question that we all ask, "Who am I and what is the meaning of my life?" The larger question that the philosopher or artist or religious leader asks is, "Who is Man?" These are questions that have no final answers. The nature of man with a capital M and the nature of each individual man continues to be disclosed to man as the world evolves. It is hinted as the artist creates new works, as the spiritual leader receives new insights, as the philosopher shapes new awareness, as the scientist discovers new principles, and as man conflicts and communes with other men and the natural world. Because it is a difficult problem, the search for value continues, controversy rages, and individuals flounder and seek solace in a variety of rituals or answers. Curriculum specialists seek to sidestep the difficulty of clear statements of goals. Critics continue to hammer away at these goals. This is not because either are right or wrong, but because the emergence and formulation of value requires dialogue and struggle as the world emerges. Our hurt feelings should be turned into joy because we are getting help in identifying and realizing new values in and for educational activity. But we clearly should stop trying to resolve the difficulty by finding the purpose of education or by providing teachers with simplified philosophies of education which discourage them from asking, "Who am I and why am I living like this in my classroom?" or which dissuade them from exploring the similarities and differences between the concept of man discussed in education courses and the concept of man basic to their religious beliefs. Education, if it is looked upon not simply as a profession or as a way of making a living but as a vocation in the sense of a calling, or even as an honest attempt to live fully, is one of the finest life styles for discovering again and again the nature of existence as lived—for the unearthing of value.

Clearly, one form of value is an instrumental form in terms of what it accomplishes or where it leads. But life lived has value not only because it produces something or ends somewhere. This is to turn present life into a commodity for a future state it offers. Life does have value because it gets one to tomorrow or next year. But there may be no tomorrow, and then, of course, life today would have been of no value. Life as lived, in the present moment, has its own values—you know, the "lilies of the field" and "the birds of the air."

The characteristics of educational activity described above, language, human encounter, and awe or wonder would seem to be manifestations of what might be called moral value; that is, one of the ways of valuing activity in the present moment is by asking whether the activity reflects man and his possibilities. Is this moment as we are living it the best that man is capable of? Does it reflect what I believe to be the nature of man and his encounters with the world? Does it help the student perceive the transcending possibilities in language and human encounter, the possibility of wonder and awe in the world of nature and art? Of course there are different moral value systems or views of what man is or can be, hence again the need for discourse and argument and political action. But to attract attention away from the present moment by asking only "What is being learned?" or "What are the expected outcomes?" is to remove educational activity from the moral into only the technical sphere. The valuing process, conceived in terms of means-ends evaluation, forces education into the realm of man's technique, or perhaps technique's man, and away from the realm of man's spirit as a temporal being.

Criticism of the schools and of education, which is the counterthrust necessary for the evolution of educational value, requires attention to moral values manifest in educational activity.[19] This form of criticism is not simply carping, but is penetrating evaluation by educated and disciplined people, aware of the moral dimensions of man's life in today's world. Schools of education have been deficient in that they have not trained teachers to be social or moral critics of educational activity.

Beside the sphere of moral values may be placed the sphere of aesthetic values. All more or less permanent artifacts, routines or rituals, and organizational structures may be detached from the world of use and hence be interpreted as symbols with aesthetic dimensions. Likewise all completed chunks of human activity, even though unique, may be looked back upon as having form and unity, and consequently as having aesthetic dimensions. Therefore the components of the educational environment and indeed edu-

[19] As one form of such criticism see Harvey Cox, *The Secular City* (New York: The Macmillan Company, 1965).

cational activity itself may be valued aesthetically. Two dimensions of aesthetic value are directly applicable to the educational environment and activity. First, because of its distancing from use, its ability to stand outside of the realm of technique, the object or structure or patterned activity has a form. Thus it has a sense of wholeness, of design, of harmony and balance. It may be said to have the potential for beauty. Likewise, separated from use, the object, structure, or activity becomes symbolic of the artist-creator and indeed of man and society. Symbolically it has the potential for truth in that it symbolizes the feelings, awareness, visions, and possibilities of the artist and his world. Educational activity and the environment in which it occurs may be valued for its beauty and truth. Does it reflect good design, is it harmonious, balanced? Does it symbolize what the teacher really is, and what man is or what man can be? The teacher at the end of an activity or day can ask, "Was this a beautiful day for me and for the students—balanced, harmonious, tension producing and reducing?" "Was it a day filled with truth, that is, did it symbolize what life really is and can be like?" This is an extremely significant form of valuing, and aesthetic criticism could be a powerful way of exposing what education and teaching means to teachers and administrators. Look at educational buildings or architectural structures—do they reflect man's spirit or his technique, man's freedom or his necessity? Search for beauty and truth in the materials used in classroom—they are not there. Instead will be found evidence of education's commitment to technique and the world of consumption. Observe a teacher's behavior and classroom procedures for design and harmony, for the dramatic qualities that heighten life. Infrequently is beauty found; more often, there is simply the ugliness of dead routine. Observe that same behavior as symbolic of that teacher's feelings and meanings of life. Some teaching, effective from a means-ends valuing system, is symbolic of feelings and means which should not exist in schools. Valued aesthetically, educational activity and environment take on new perspectives. Aesthetic criticism is a form of evaluation infrequently brought to bear on education. It is also a disciplined activity, requiring an educated eye, a sense of design, and an awareness of modern man. Schools of education do little to encourage aesthetic forms of valuing and criticism.

The central, most significant, part of curriculum, however, is not value but educational activity itself. Activity takes place within an environment. The designing and fabrication of this environment is the task of the curriculum specialist. Indeed, it might be appropriate to refer to him as a curriculum designer. Discussions of value have consequences in the educational environments that result. To ask, "What is the purpose of educa-

tion?" is to ask about the characteristics of the school as a place to live.[20]
But to ask, "What moral and aesthetic values should be manifest in educational activity?" is also to ask about the characteristics of the school as a
place to live.

To build an environment which structures educational activity means to
select content from the whole, wide, wonderful world and to make it available for students. So conceived, content is that which is available in the
classroom for educational activity. This includes man-made objects, aspects
of the natural world grouped or organized in certain ways, symbol or language systems, and usages or social conventions. In fact, educational content becomes a selection of man's culture, thus creating a limited culture for
the student. But to keep the image clear, it is necessary to use culture the
way Tillich uses it. He reminds those who have been over-conditioned by
the behavioral scientist that the biologist uses it differently: "Culture, cul-
tura, is that which takes care of something, keeps it alive, and makes it
grow."[21] The curriculum designer fabricates an educational environment
which takes care of students, keeps them alive, and makes them grow. The
teacher, to use technical language, has an ambiguous role. On the one
hand, he represents one part of the content, a part of the culture. As a conditioned being, the teacher brings certain language patterns and behavioral
usages into the classroom. Thus he is part of the technique and is a tech-
nician. But as a representative of man's spirit, of man's freedom, he must
also be a free agent in order to realize moral and aesthetic values in educational activity. It is in the teacher and in the teacher's education and continuing education that the major struggle between man's techniques and
man's spirit is waged. This is what makes teaching such a significant life
activity today, for the teacher epitomizes more sharply than anyone else this
twentieth-century struggle, engaged as he is in the confrontation of youth
becoming aware of a destiny and a social group trying to determine what
that destiny will be. The size of institutionalized education makes the
struggle even more significant, for educational organizations, administrative
structures and styles, and educational materials—all technical devices to
achieve ends efficiently—help shape the course of the teacher's struggle.

The design of educational environment and activity requires technical
skill. It is in the design and fabrication of the environment that the means-
end qualities of traditional curricular thought bear fruit. The most excit-

[20] R. S. Peters, *Authority, Responsibility, and Education* (London: Allen and
Unwin, 1962).
[21] Paul Tillich, *Systematic Theology*, Vol. III (Chicago: The University of Chicago
Press, 1963).

ing evidence of this is seen in the vigor with which the new media specialists have taken up the cry, "Define your objective behaviorally!" and have
adopted the label, "learning technology," as they begin to build instruments
and systems for instruction.[22] In the construction of new materials and devices, learning theory has its maximum application in education. The use
of theories of learning and behavior for the construction of materials is like
the use of physical theories in the design of new buildings, roadways, instruments of communication, and weapons. They change the characteristics
of the environment in which we live, and bring forth new responses from
those who live in that environment.

Technology in the schools makes three significant contributions to the
educational environment. The first is the externalization of a language system into tangible form. Textbooks and information books are tangible, and
they serve to put the student into the same language community with scientists or scholars or workers. New developments in programming increase
the opportunity to externalize dialogue, and thus increase the possibility of
starting the student on one of the paths of language transcendence, for example, language laboratories. Next, technology increases the opportunity
for personal encounters via telephone hookups, television, tapes, letters, and
finally by way of the arts, wherein the student has distinct opportunities for
the "Who am I?" comparison, as he is projected into the lives and feelings
of others. Third, as extensions of man's senses[23] technology makes possible
new confrontations of the student with the non-technical and increases the
opportunity for the experience of awe and wonder. Again art and poetry
are examples, the microprojector is another, as can be television and film.
The media specialists lose some of their power when they seek to install all
media into existing techniques of education. As McLuhan has said, the
medium is the message, opening up new vistas of man and his possibilities.
The media specialist could also ask, "What does this new technology suggest about man and his possibilities?" and "What kind of educational value
can it have in schools?" not simply "How can it facilitate learning?" As
Mumford pointed out, the neo-technique is to serve man, not to be served
by man.[24] Hence technical developments for education must seek to realize
moral and aesthetic values in educational activity as well as technical values.
Only in this way can concern for man remain uppermost.

Of course, the educational environment, and consequently educational
activity, is limited by time, space, and money. So choices must be made
among values to be manifested and content to be included in the classroom.

[22] Robert Glaser, op. cit.

[23] Marshall McLuhan, op. cit.

[24] Lewis Mumford, op. cit.

Some values and content are rather universally accepted. For instance, all agree that one educative activity is reading. Some argument about reading is technical argument; for example, which method is most economical? Hopefully, from now to the end of time more efficient methods will evolve that will give teachers greater choice as they teach reading. The search for *the* way to design reading activity is absurd. The search for the most economic way is not, but economics is a subvalue within technique. The argument over text or trade book is perhaps really an argument about the book content of the educational environment. But other aspects of educational content do not find universal agreement. Here, then, the public discussions about aims or ends is part of a vast ideological[25] struggle over control of educational content. This ideological struggle is a reflection of the changing social scene, in terms of new conditions of social life, but also in terms of new social groups gaining ascendency in the power hierarchy. The ideological struggle is necessary as a form of value clarification as the society evolves and meets new problems and possibilities. It is necessary for the evolution of new educational forms and structures. No person, not even the professional educator, can be omniscient about the future characteristics of the society and the consequent shape of educational environments and activities. Consequently the educator needs to accept and participate in constructive social criticism about educational content and to engage in the political process which is man's way of building his social environment.

What is the role of the curricular specialist in this political process? As the fabricator and designer of educational environments, he seeks in the school a just environment for all members of the society. Tillich states that "justice is the uniting function in the individual man and in the social group."[26] The curriculum maker must strive to create an educative environment which represents the values and valued content of all involved social groups, including, as one involved group, the students. The content of the school has shifted as the political process has indicated that now one group, now another, needed attention or gained control. When no one else speaks for an important or neglected group or set of values, then the educator must. He must represent none, yet all. To the extent that he takes unjustified sides, he ruins his effectiveness as the educational adjudicator. As dispassionately as the judge in the law court, he must listen to all sides, including the prophets, and seek to build a just educative environment. Today the curriculum maker is being helped by others who finally care enough about

[25] See Karl Mannheim, *Ideology and Utopia* (New York: Harcourt, Brace and Company, 1936).

[26] Paul Tillich, *Love, Power, and Justice* (New York: Oxford University Press, 1954), p. 55.

the schools to help in the construction of a just and moral educational environment. The curriculum designer is thus freed from the overburdening responsibility of doing all, and gradually he can begin to see the forest as well as the trees. This is an opportunity for which he has perhaps been waiting and which he should by all means use. The study of curriculum is really the heart and soul of the study of education. All of man's knowledge, wisdom, and skill is required to build a just educational environment. The study of curriculum can be and should be a great liberal and liberating study, for through it the specialist must come to grips with the great social and intellectual problems of today. The study of curriculum need not be the search for curriculum theory, although eventually a theory or theories may emerge. The study of curriculum need not be labeled as a profession, for prestige follows from work, not labels. Is it possible, now that we are partially freed from the vision-hindering busy work, that we can begin to make efforts to grasp the overall design of curriculum and to see how man's evolving techniques can be made subservient to man's evolving spirit? Educational environment and activity in the schools are symbolic of what man is today and what he wants to be tomorrow. The design of these symbols is a great art. The study of curriculum should be a preparation for this artistry.